YOU ARE ABOUT TO ENTER THE KITCHEN OF THE BLACK SWAN AT HELMSLEY

New and Classic Recipes
from
John Benson Smith
Chef de Cuisine

The Black Swan

HELMSLEY

TO PAUL GILL
whose leadership, guidance, professionalism,
insight and expertise inspires us all ...

WITH SPECIAL THANKS
to all 'the Team' — the Staff and the Kitchen
Brigade to whom I have given a hard time
(and shall continue to do so)

*"Food should have the Qualities of Life
Gentleness, Lightness, Fun and Sincerity"
'MICHAEL QUINN' M.B.E.*

Grateful acknowledgement is given to Edward Arnold (Publishers) for permission to reproduce general information on basic sauces and stocks (including recipes for White Sauce, Velouté, Brown Sauce, Demi-Glace, Roast Gravy and Hollandaise) from 'Practical Cookery' by V. Ceserani and R. Kinton.

The Black Swan is one of the many luxury hotels owned by Trusthouse Forte.
We acknowledge the assistance and information given in producing this book.
We are grateful to the people mentioned and for the recipes given and used.

Published by Highgate Publications (Beverley) Ltd.
24 Wylies Road, Beverley, HU17 7AP
Telephone (0482) 866826

Produced by
B.A. Press, 2-4 Newbegin, Lairgate, Beverley, HU17 8EG
Telephone (0482) 882232

ISBN 0-948929-25-1

British Library Cataloguing in Publication Data
Smith, John Benson, 1958-
    The kitchen of the Black Swan.
    1. Catering establishments. Food — Recipes
    I. Title
    641.5'7

ISBN 0-948929-25-1

Front Cover Portrait John Benson Smith — Fiona Scott

Original Design Work — Mike Herringshaw

CONTENTS

"As far as cuisine is concerned, one must read
everything in order to retain in the end just a little bit"
'FERNAND POINT'

FOREWORD

*What I wanted was a Chef, but I ended up with a good friend —
simply John Smith but who would have noticed the Chef at The
Black Swan with such a name? So he used his full name — John
Benson Smith.*

*We strive to achieve the impossible — a frequently heard phrase is
"Excellence is not enough". The most common bond between John
and myself is the pursuit of excellence.*

*My mood is affected on arrival at the Hotel, if I find a sweet paper
outside the front, a geranium that has not been dead-headed or the ice
melted in the ice bucket of Welcoming Fruit Wine on Reception Desk
— I could go on . . .*

Well John is of a similar mind.

*I suppose nowadays an unusual approach is John's determination to
cater for the Guest, whilst others follow fashion, whims and so on . . .*

*John Benson Smith is quiet and unassuming, his personality is
revealed in the pleasure he derives from his kitchen. I hope you will
agree and that after reading this book you too, will have found a
friend as I did.*

Paul Gill

JOHN BENSON
SMITH

John Benson Smith with Paul Gill

I rarely measure as I cook. I have imagined a reader who understands 'the basics' of cookery and I have given some thought to cost, availability of products and the limitations of domestic kitchens.

I believe the whole point in being a Chef is doing things others would not dare do, never being afraid to alter or adjust. My hope is that these recipes and thoughts will amuse those who will never try them, and inspire those who do time and time again, enjoy them.

Memories and events are brought to mind when hearing pieces of music from one's past. The same, I feel, can be said of recipes and dishes. Collected here are a few of my favourites. I hope you enjoy my ideas and inspirations.

Let your eyes arrange it. Your taste decide it.

Best Wishes

John Benson Smith

A CHEF

The position of Chef encompasses the various abilities, within the bounds of the kitchen, to be an architect, butcher, cook, baker, artist, builder, accountant, chemist, designer, engineer, scientist, dietician and psychologist and above all a great diplomat in his own right, coupled with last but not least, an incurable love for food and a life long ambition to learn.

Each has his own personality, which is reflected in his style of cooking, and that of his unique brigade.

His menus are nothing but card and print, his expression from beginning to end is cooked, arranged, garnished and presented, and placed upon "the plate".

The food should be simple, the best raw ingredients used, and the basics firmly understood.

To create a good dish of repute for a day is easy, to do the same for a month or year, is difficult.

John Benson Smith

My OPINION

Things I did ten years ago on menus I would not dream of doing now. Over a period of time you develop your own taste, style and techniques and formulations, and opinions of your own and others cooking. One is rarely happy with creations, since you strive for higher levels than the dish before.

Very little in cuisine is new, it has all been discovered before in one form or another.

If you can invent two new dishes in five years, you are doing well.

What is important, is using your creativity and imagination to develop tastes, textures and ideas. If I form a good dish or recipe, I stick to it. Volkswagen didn't fit six doors to its car one day then three the next.

I feel people want to return to experience a "classic" that they have enjoyed before. Reliability and consistency are firm foundations on which to build. Try to perfect rather than change for changes sake. The basic aim should be to produce wholesome, attractive tasty food which has been tried and tested beforehand. Guests are not to be regarded as guinea pigs.

I view style in food as a big wheel, rotating through the decades of fashion, slowly moving from one whim to another.

The French generally stick to their styles and renowned dishes and cuisines, where we, in this country, search for our 'unknown cuisine' when it sits ignored right in front of our faces.

Above all, work clean and tidy, believe in youth and the Chefs of tomorrow.

WE ARE BRITISH, SO LET US BE PROUD OF OUR OWN ACHIEVEMENTS!

John Benson Smith

COUNTRY CUISINE

AN ADAPTATION

The cold kitchen ranges, grills and ovens are lit by the night porter for the beginning of the day. Cool, bare, lifeless areas waiting the start of today (always different from yesterday and tomorrow).

The early Chef starts his day's tasks unlocking fridges and rooms, surveying the morning's products, enquiring his Breakfast numbers, checking his hotplate, greets the milkman with an order ... minutes later removes his croissants from the pastry oven. Finishes fruit arrangements, squeezing of fresh juices, splits kidneys, passes the unsalted butter for a mug of sweet tea ... the phone rings in the Head Chef's office, parcel of kippers arrives fresh from 'a Scottish loch' ... bowls, basins, seasonings, clean board and oven cloths discovered.

The Menu emerges from morning bustle. Smoked Salmon carved for a Speciality and melon cut into a fresh wedge, an egg boiled, bacon grilled, black pudding salted, the parsley rummaged for in the fridge, cream poured into a porridge, plates warmed.

Kitchen Porter arrives, as important as any other member, he starts his chores, sorting, cleaning, moving and carting ... to the butcher's for fresh sausages ordered for tomorrow. Collects a newspaper on his way back, unloads and stores the daily bread, fills his sinks and clatters pans and trays.

The Sous Chef appears, fills his stockpot with water and fresh veal bones, greets the early Chef who now pulls in the clutch and changes gear, the orders come in thick and fast (if he requires help he will ask). The Sous peels his fresh vegetables, chops and seals a garlic, runs his steel up and down his favourite knife.

A figure appears at the kitchen door to see the Head Chef with no appointment, the Sous Chef sends him packing.

The Saucier Chef hurries to his section grunting "Good Morning", completes his daily wine order and chops Turbot Bones and Butter and reviews his work load, grabs a coffee, bones, rolls, trusses and trims and skins the morning fresh meat then barks as his junior arrives late, sleepy and with no hat.

Being late the Pastry Chef, unbeknownst to all, has slipped into his room, purées his marinaded fruits, starts his oven, mislays his scale pan and unpacks chocolate moulds.

The fish stock is complete, the butter clarified, more hares to sauté, spinach blanched for the dinner's terrine.

The Breakfast finishes, wiping down, sweeping and mopping commences.

All the 'misenplus' and preparation from yesterday is changed.

'The Chef' materialises: immediately the phone rings. The Sous Chef meets him in the office to exchange notes, make calls to and from specific suppliers enquiring, prompting and questioning. Lambs. Lettuce. Foie Gras. Smoked Salmon and Peaches, orders are rattled off for the day.

The Menus are completed, events, functions, appointments and meetings are surveyed.

Greeting his Brigade, grunting, smiling, pushing with comments, instruction, anger, warmth and determination, he gets bored with the office, attends to a Junior's cuts and burns, inspects produce for a journalist's visit and demonstration.

Bones out fowl chatting with Chef de Parti discussing moments and characters from France.

The Apprentice appears with the day's post. House Numbers and Memos.

'The Chef' barks "Why hasn't the Salad Box arrived?" "Why are the copper pans in the wrong place — again?"

The Saucier passes and creams the luncheon soup. What has the Vegetable Chef prepared for the day? The new lamb arrives, it's checked and inspected. The staff meal is ready ... preparation time is nearly over. Reality is here, the waiters arrive, bookings are checked, melba toast completed, and a little burnt.

Restaurant Manager and Sous Chef admire and chat over the new cheeses, the oil is filtered for the day, celery trimmed, apples polished, discussion again of the menus, checking of sections, final tastings and seasoning and second opinion on a sorbet flavour. Lettuces picked, dressings whisked, cream whipped and carrots flowered.

The first customers arrive, an order taken, a Junior Chef hurries to turn up a gas and flame. The calm waiter hands 'The Chef' the first order, he shouts out the instructions, all departments answer with the noise, the tempo quickens, doors open and shut, shouts start, a terrine is sliced and oranges segmented, a duck breast sealed and salmon baked in pastry. The first cheque hangs on the board, a pan clatters. The Pastry Chef whisks with vigour, the speed increases, orders appear, instructions barked, memories engage and minds are active.

Vegetables tossed in butter to coincide with the Saucier's Duck, steam fills an area as ladle is too hot to touch, a supplier arrives, the phone rings, veal stock added to a flaming brandy.
The Chef chases a waiter to wipe a drop of sauce from a plate's rim, visitors walk through on a tour.
Desserts are served, the Pastry Chef hurries to the garden for fresh mint to decorate. Knives chop and slice amongst the clatter and shout: the Saucier is in need of a special pan. A unique soup warmed, a small crowd form as a new dish is completed.
Mixing, tasting, slicing, smoke charcoals the air, presentation, orders slacken.
The Restaurant Manager says goodbye to the customer.
Behind the Kitchen doors the day has just begun.

John Benson Smith

"There can be nothing better than cooking things you have grown in your own garden; nothing better than sitting down with friends, talking and laughing over food from ingredients you have made yourself."
YORKSHIRE POST
John Benson Smith

THE KITCHEN
BRIGADE

JOHN BENSON SMITH	Chef de Cuisine
ALEC HOWARD	Head Chef
NIGEL WRIGHT	Sous Chef
JOANNE WARD	Vegetable Chef
ADAM RICHARDSON	Pastry Chef
MATTHEW BENSON SMITH	Larder Chef
ALAN MILES	Pastry Comis Chef
MICHAEL STEVENSON	Sauce Chef
SHARON SMITH	Apprentice Chef
JENNIFER BULMER	Apprentice Chef
LEE PURCELL	Apprentice Chef
SIMON RICHARDSON	Demi Chef
JOHN JOHNSON)	Kitchen
DENNIS DALE)	Porter &
GILLIAN SEWEL)	Assistants

Working at Speed

EGON RONAY RECOMMENDED RESTAURANT
*"Splendid Sauces, Spot-on Seasoning and first rate
presentation make for excellent eating"*

TO COMMENCE

STARTERS

SALAD GOURMANDE

RIEVAULX SALAD

WARM DUCK SALAD WITH GREEN BEANS

MANGE TOUT SALAD WITH CHICKEN LIVERS AND BACON

CRAB AND SMOKED SALMON TERRINE

MARJOLAINE DE FOIE GRAS

SMOKED SALMON WITH ASPARAGUS MOUSSE

HAM SOUFFLE

TERRINE OF DUCK WITH PISTACHIO NUTS

MARROW SOUFFLE

PEARLS OF AVOCADO WITH PRAWNS AND MUSTARD

BAKED AVOCADO PEAR

PICKLED MELON

TRIO OF EGG SHELLS

SWEET ONION FLAN

FRIED EGGS WITH TOMATO AND VINEGAR

CHEEKY LOBSTER FOR SUMMER

VINAIGRETTE

TIP:
To Clean Copper
Mix equal amounts of salt. flour and tomato purée together.
spread on and leave. wash off and polish.

STARTERS

SALAD GOURMANDE
Serves Four (Grand Salad)

Meaning "The best Salad" which would be plated and really requires no accompaniment but bread. Would be served as and when required.
My salad is dedicated to Louis Outhier, the world's finest creator of salads.

Ingredients:

1	Avocado Pear (ripe)
small bowl	Pickled Endives & Salad (Chicory, Lambs Tongues, Curly Endive, Radoccio etc.)
1 lb	Lobster (Whitby) (cooked)
1	Apple (Red, English and sliced)
4	Asparagus (thin) (half cooked/blanched)
4	Cherry Tomatoes (inside removed)
4 sprigs	Mint
1 sprig	Chervil
4	Wild Mushrooms
4	Radish
1 tsp	Caviar

Dressing:

1	Part Red Wine	) Mix
1	Part Wine Vinegar	) all
¼	Part Dijon Mustard	) together,
7	Parts Olive Oil	) adding
	Salt/Pepper/	) Oil
	Tarragon	) finally.

Method:

Wash all Endives in cold water.
Skin and slice Avocado.
Slice cooked Lobster Tail.
Quickly sauté Wild Mushrooms.
Place in a 4″ ring on centre of plate.
Layer alternately with Endives, Apple, Avocado, Asparagus, etc.
Compact and serve dressing on top or separately.
Remove ring and serve.

Garnish:

Caviar, Mint and Radish Flower.

"A plain white plate is the basis for success"

RIEVAULX SALAD
Serves Two

Named after the local Abbey

Ingredients:

10 fl.oz/250ml	Whipped Double Cream (seasoned)
2	Sprigs of Mint
60g	Gravalax Salmon (cut into thin strips)
1oz/30g	Picked Endives
4 tsp	Laverbread (seaweed)
Half	Fresh Cucumber (peeled)
1 tsp	Caviar

Method:

Place the four 3" diameter rings onto the service plates.
In the base of each put some picked Endives.

Mix the Gravalax with two thirds of the whipped cream, ¾ fill each ring with the mixture. Compact well with a spatula.

Make a thin layer of laverbread on top and finish the remaining space with more whipped cream. Smooth over the top with a spatula.

Gently run a small hot knife around the inside of the rings and remove them.

Slice the cucumber into two halves lengthways. Make four small fans to top each Gateau and slice the remainder thinly. Put the half slices overlapping around the Gateauxs.

Garnish:

A little Caviar on the top and a mint leaf.

Surround the Salad with a little French Dressing and serve.

JOHN BENSON SMITH
"A real expert at presentation, a joy to see and how neat and tidy whilst cooking"
Rosemary Gray, Eggleston Hall

WARM DUCK SALAD WITH GREEN BEANS
Serves Two

Ingredients:

2 x 8oz/225g	Breast of Duck (cooked and cut into strips, warm)
2oz/50g	Julienne (strips) of Fine Beans (blanched) Endives (picked)
1	Peeled, sliced Apple (blanched)

Apple Dressing:

2 parts	Olive Oil
1 part	Apple Juice
1 part	White Wine Vinegar

Seasoning:

¾oz/20g	Tomato Concassée Chervil

Method:

Quickly seal off the Duck Breast in a hot pan. Finish cooking in an oven for 4 - 5 minutes. Remove from pan when cooked and allow to cool slightly.

Pick the Endives and wash.

Prepare Dressing by mixing all the ingredients together.

Blanch the Fine Beans.

Place a metal pastry ring in the centre of the plate, slice the Duck Breast and put on the base. On top place Endives, nappe over a little dressing.

Place the Fine Beans, cut into Julienne (strips) on the top. Surround the dish with remainder of dressing and sliced (blanched) Apple.

Garnish with the Tomato Concassée and fresh Chervil herb.

N.B. *The days of frozen Margrat French Duck Breast are, 'thank goodness', now over with the arrival of Cumbrian Ducks in particular being a better quality product.*

MANGE TOUT SALAD WITH CHICKEN LIVER AND BACON
Serves Four

Ingredients:

12oz/350g	Mange Tout
6 tbsp	Groundnut, Sunflower or Hazelnut Oil
4 tbsp	White Wine Vinegar
6	Chicken Livers (cubed with stringy parts removed)
	Salt and Black Pepper
6	Very thin rashers of Streaky Bacon (cut into strips)
	Bacon Fat or extra Oil (if necessary)
16oz/450g	Small Bread (diced)

Method:

Have 4 warm individual serving dishes ready. Top, tail and string the mange tout. Cook them to the state of tenderness you prefer. Drain and put into a warm bowl. Mix the oil and vinegar together and add to the mange tout, keep warm.

Season the livers with salt and pepper. Cook the strips of bacon in their own fat using a little extra fat or oil if necessary. Try to get them crisp and curly. Remove with slotted spoon, then fry the bread dice until golden. Drain and add to the bacon strips.

Finally cook the liver pieces in the remaining fat, adding more fat or oil if necessary. The liver should be pink inside. Put the bacon and bread back in the fat for a few seconds to warm through slightly.

Arrange the mange tout, hot liver, bacon and bread dice in the serving dishes and serve immediately.

Garnish with herbs.

"The unique, genial and personable Paul Gill offers a gourmet dining room to rival a far larger establishment"
Tamba Bay, Tribune Times

CRAB AND SMOKED SALMON TERRINE
Serves Four

Ingredients:

4oz/100g	Smoked Salmon (sliced for lining terrine)
1 x 1lb/450g	Crab (cooked)
½oz/15g	Gelatine Powder*
	Juice of 1 Lemon
¼pt	Mayonnaise
¼pt	Double Cream
2oz/⅛ dl	Tomato Sauce
	Seasoning

*Gelatine I have a particular dislike for, this can be replaced with melted butter

Method:

Line a terrine mould with the sliced smoked salmon. Mince the crab meat, taken from the shell, in a food processor. Dissolve the gelatine in a little lemon juice. Mix the other ingredients together well. Add the gelatine mixture, fill the terrine, cover with clingfilm and refrigerate for 24 hours with weights placed on top.

Turn out and slice, an electric carving knife is ideal.

Garnish with fresh raddish. Serve with a little salad leaves and brown bread.

"I was sent to borrow and ask for chicken tips, left-handed screwdrivers, glass hammers, bullets for the lobster gun, etc. Apprentice jokes are things that stick in your mind. You can read their situations, you were in it a little while ago yourself, but now you want them to learn how a melon grows on a plant, not if Tottenham beat Sheffield United"
John Benson Smith

Waiting to take an order

Terrine of Duckling

TERRINE MARJOLAINE de FOIE GRAS
Serves Eight

In the style of Louis Outhier

Ingredients:

2lb/900g	Cooked Fresh Duck/Goose Liver (Foie Gras)
1 or 2	Truffles, finely sliced (optional) !!!
1	Egg White
1oz	Flour
2oz	Butter (creamed)
2oz	Almonds (shredded)
Pinch	Salt
¼ Pint	Chicken Consommé

Method:

To make the Almond Crust —
Lightly beat the egg white, then beat in the flour, creamed butter, almonds and salt. Spread in a ¼ inch layer on a well buttered, chilled 16 x 10 inch baking tray. Using a sharp knife, divide the paste into 4 strips of 4 x 10 inch. This must be done now as the cooked pastry is extremely fragile.

Bake in a pre-heated oven at Gas Mark 4 (190°C, 375°F) for 10-12 minutes. Cool.

Divide the cooked foie gras into 3 equal portions. Spread one-third evenly on a strip of almond crust, cover with another layer of crust and so on. If you are using truffles, arrange them in an even layer in the centre layer of foie gras.

Press down lightly and smooth the sides with a spatula. Chill for 6 hours.

Garnish with tomato rose, chopped tarragon aspic and lemon leaves.

Serve with chilled chicken consommé.

SMOKED SALMON WITH ASPARAGUS MOUSSE
Serves Four

Ingredients:

10oz/275g	Asparagus
1	Leaf Gelatine
1 tbsp	Sherry
5 fl.oz/125ml	Double Cream (half whipped)
	Seasoning
8 Slices	Smoked Salmon
1 Sprig	Fresh Dill
	Tomato Rose

Sauce:

5 fl.oz/125ml	Double Cream
5 fl.oz/125ml	Yogurt
	Juice of a Lime
	Seasoning

Method:

Dissolve the gelatine in the sherry, liquidise the precooked asparagus (if you use tinned, ensure it is well drained), mix with the cream. Season and add the gelatine mix. Place a spoonful of the mix into the centre of smoked salmon slices and form neat parcels. Place in the fridge.

Mix the cream and yogurt together with the lime juice, add the seasoning.

Place the parcels into the plates, garnish with the tips of asparagus, fresh dill and tomato rose.
Pour a pool of sauce at the side of each parcel.

Garnish:

Asparagus Tips with fresh Dillweed and Fennel.

"We present our Foie Gras in the display of a hedgehog" **John Benson Smith**

"Recognition of the high standard displayed in the management and presentation of your cheeseboard. We applaud you."
John Freestone, Dairy Crest
Symbol of Excellence Award

HAM SOUFFLÉ
Serves Four

Ingredients:

1oz	Unsalted Butter, plus a little more for greasing
3oz	Flour (plain)
½pt/300ml	Double Cream
2oz/50g	Grated Gruyère Cheese
4oz/100g	Ham (cooked and finely minced)
4	Eggs (separated)
	Cayenne Pepper

Method:

Melt the butter in a pan and add in the flour, stirring continuously. When blended add the cream a little at a time. Simmer for a few minutes until the sauce is thick and smooth. Leave to cool, then mix in the cheese, ham and well beaten egg yolks and season to taste with cayenne pepper.

Beat the egg whites until very stiff and fold into the mixture. Turn into a buttered soufflé mould and bake in a moderate oven, 180°C, 350°F, Gas Mark 4 for 25-30 minutes until well risen and golden brown.

Garnish with wedges of orange.

Serve immediately with cucumber relish.

TERRINE OF DUCK WITH PISTACHIO NUTS
Serves Four

A recipe personally given to me by Michael Quinn, a true example of his approach to English food.

Ingredients:

2	Breasts of Duck
2	Egg Whites
	Seasoning
¼pt/150ml	Double Cream

1 measure each of:
Maderia
Sherry
Brandy

2oz/50g	Peeled Pistachio Nuts
	Fresh blanched Spinach

Method:

Marinade the Breast of Duck overnight in the alcohol, cover with film and place in a fridge.

Place the Breasts in a food processor and reduce to a purée with the egg whites and pass through a fine sieve. Season and add to the cream.

Pour into a terrine mould lined with thin freshly blanched spinach, push finely chopped pistachio nuts into the mixture and cover with spinach.

Bake in a bain marie of water for 1 hour 10 minutes on Gas Mark 4 with a lid on. The more water in the bain marie the less chance the Terrine souffles. Check it is cooked by inserting a needle or kitchen fork into the centre of the terrine, leave for 30 seconds, withdraw and place against your wrist to feel if it is hot and cooked.

Refrigerate for 24 hours.
Turn out and garnish with a little salad, slice with an electric carving knife, and serve with toast.

"Cumbria now produces some of the finest ducks, in my opinion, in the world"

MARROW SOUFFLÉ
Serves Four

Total myths are souffle secrets, practise with confidence!

Ingredients:

2oz/50g	Butter
1	Small Onion (minced)
2oz/50g	Plain Flour
	Seasoning
1 tbsp	Herbs (chopped)
10 fl.oz	Milk
8oz/275ml	Marrow (peeled, seeded and grated)
2 tbsp	Soured Cream
4	Egg Yolks
5	Egg Whites

Method:

Melt the butter in a saucepan, add the onion and fry until it is golden brown.
Stir in the flour and cook for one minute, stirring.
Remove the pan from the heat and stir in seasoning to taste, add the herbs.
Incorporate the milk slowly, return to the heat and cook until thickened and smooth.
Remove from the heat and pass through a fine sieve and cool.
Stir in the marrow, soured cream and egg yolks, cool again.

Beat the egg whites separately until they will hold a stiff peak, fold them into the marrow mixture. Spoon into a buttered 3 pint straight sided soufflé dish and bake in a fairly hot oven 190°C, 350°F, Gas Mark 5 for 35 to 40 minutes or until golden brown and risen.

Garnish:

Blanched marrow and onion cooked in tomato juice.

Serve immediately with a sauce of crab, cheese and parsley.

"Attitude is the number one problem you encounter and those who don't accept correction, or advice, plus those who don't want change or to learn, and let's not forget those scared ones who might be seen to achieve things, or come and help: each catering person should have an IQ test and certificate for attitude — it would help us all!"
John Benson Smith

PEARLS OF AVOCADO WITH PRAWNS AND MUSTARD
Serves Four

"A recipe reminding me of Brighton sea front and long walks"

Ingredients:

2	Avocado Pear Pearls (use a Parisienne Scoop)
1 tsp	English Mustard
½pt/300ml	Cream (Whipping)
	Seasoning
4oz/100g	Peeled Prawns
1oz/25g	Chopped Onion
1oz/25g	Butter

Method:

Cut the ripe Avocado Pear in half lengthwise. Remove the stone, scoop out the pearls of flesh. Retain the skin and flesh.

Sweat the onion in a little butter, add the prawns, mustard and cream. Boil to reduce and thicken.
Add the Avocado flesh, and season.

Lightly warm the skin and fill with the mixture.

Garnish with a tomato petal, picked parsley and sprinkle with paprika.

"Louis Outhier smiled and chattered in French. It happened on many occasions. I understood nothing, but really everything. He bumped the wall one night in his funny tiny Fiat car, he didn't notice or react, probably creating for the year 2000 in his mind."
John Benson Smith

BAKED AVOCADO PEAR
Serves Two

Ingredients:

2	Egg Yolks
2	Israeli Avocado Pears (ripe)
12oz/350g	Puff Pastry
3oz/75g	Butter (seasoned with chopped garlic)
6	Black Olives
2	Bay Leaves
2	Cloves
	Strips of Carrot and Celery soaked in iced water

Method:

Select a ripe Avocado Pear. Remove the skin from the stalk downwards. Place to one side.

Roll out your pastry to 2mm thickness to adequately cover the pear. Cut the pear horizontally in the area of the stone and remove. Place in the well a pearl of garlic butter the size of the stone. Replace the top and cover neatly with the pastry, forming creases towards the bottom. Cut a flat out of the bottom of the Avocado so it sits vertically.

Design and place two pastry leaves on the top of the pear, securing with a clove. Brush with egg yolk and season. Place on a baking tray and bake in a hot oven for 15-20 minutes until browned.
Remove from the oven and serve.

Garnish with a bay leaf, black olives and strips of carrot and celery.

PICKLED MELON
Serves Six

Ideal for cool summer picnics

Ingredients:

1	Ripe Melon, peeled, seeded and cut into 1″ small cubes or pearls (preferably ogen)
1pt	Pickle Stock made from a mixture of approximately ⅓pt each of Sherry, Light Syrup and Orange Juice, (vinegar to taste)
2 tbsp	Sherry
6oz	Fresh Summer Fruits (cherries, berries, segments, etc.)
2	Cloves
8	Fresh Mint Leaves
2	Peppercorns
Half	Cucumber. Cut skin in 2″ strips (discard flesh)

Method:

Place the melon into a sterilised preserving jar, add the summer fruits (raspberries, strawberries are best avoided as they tend to disintegrate and disperse colour). Add the pickle stock and other ingredients, very gently mix together. Seal the jar lid.
Turn upside down if leak proof and refrigerate for a minimum of 2 hours. Garnish and decorate lightly.
Serve.

Keeps refrigerated for 5 days. You may find that you may wish to alter or adjust the recipe to your own taste.

Serve from the jar.

"A night at the Black Swan was firmly one we shall long remember for comfort and excellent food".
James Davis, Daily Express

"A recipe best adjusted to your own individual taste" **John Benson Smith**

TRIO OF EGG SHELLS
Truffle and Scrambled Eggs; Fine Caviar and Sabayon; Salmon Roe with Lobster Mousse
Serves Four

Ingredients:

12 x	Egg Shells (tops removed)
4 x	Whole Eggs
4 x	Yolks
Remaining 4 x	Whites 4 eggs re-used
50g	Soft Butter
200ml/7floz	Cream
150g	Lobster Meat
100ml	Whipped Cream
	Salmon Keta

Method:

Oeuve au Caviar

Whisk yolks (x 4) over Bain Marie (hot water) with 50ml of White Wine rapidly until ribbon stage is achieved.
Season well. Add 25g of soft butter to finish.
Pour into four of the empty egg shells, half fill them. Whisk 7 fl.oz (200ml) of cream until stiff with a little cayenne pepper and salt.
Pipe with a straight nozzle onto the top of the egg shell in a spiral fashion, ensuring the Sabayon does not spill out. Top with a small teaspoon of Caviar on each and place in the egg cup ready to serve.

Lobster Mousse

Chop with a knife (or food processor) 150g of Lobster Meat (cooked) until very fine. Season well with salt and pepper. Fold in 100ml of whipped cream. Pipe into four empty egg shells filling over the top again in a spiral fashion.
Top each with a teaspoon of Salmon Keta. Place in egg cups ready to serve.

Scrambled Egg and Truffle

Melt gently 5oz(20g) butter in a pan, add 4 well beaten eggs. Season well. Cook gently until light and fluffy and finish with 1 fl.oz (50ml) of cream and 1oz(4gm) of chopped truffle.
Spoon carefully into egg shells in egg cups.

Place a small doily on all 4 plates and the three different eggs on each plate.

SWEET ONION FLAN
Serves Four

Ingredients:

	Olive Oil
5oz/125g	Small Diced Carrots
2lb/400g	Spanish Onion (shredded)
Pinch	Fresh Thyme
	Seasoning
8oz/225g	Diced Mushrooms
8	Large Cabbage Leaves
2	Eggs (lightly beaten)
1-2 tbsp	Skimmed Milk Powder dissolved in
¾pt/450ml	Water

Method:

Preheat oven to Gas Mark 3 (170°C, 325°F).

Moisten the bottom of a thick bottomed pan with olive oil. Add the diced carrots and cook over a moderate heat for 5 minutes. Stir and add the onion, thyme and seasoning. Cover for 10 minutes and sweat. Stir in the diced mushrooms and cook for a further 5 minutes.

Meanwhile cut out the thick ribs from the cabbage leaves and blanch in salted water for 4-5 minutes, then plunge into iced water to refresh. Drain and dry with kitchen paper.

Combine the lightly beaten egg with the dissolved skimmed milk powder and season to taste. Stir in the cooked vegetables.

Line a 7 inch cake tin with blanched cabbage leaves leaving enough spare to fold over. Fill the lined tin with the milk and vegetable mixture. Fold over the cabbage leaves and cover with tin foil.

Place in a bain marie of water and boil. Transfer to the oven and bake for 50 minutes. Remove from the oven and place in the freezer for 20 minutes.
Turn out and serve.

Garnish with roast baby onion salad.

"I know more trainees, assistants, deputy and general managers than head chefs in the industry — I'm glad. Negative chefs are dangerous — you have to think what will their apprentices turn out like"
John Benson Smith

FRIED EGGS WITH TOMATO AND VINEGAR
Serves Four

Ingredients:

8 Large Brown Eggs
2oz/50g Butter
8 Tomatoes
8 tsp Wine Vinegar
Seasoning
Parsley

Method:

Plunge the tomatoes into boiling water for 10 seconds then place in iced water and remove the skins. Squeeze gently to remove all seeds and finely chop with a little parsley.

Rub the frying pan with salt and wipe clean to remove all traces. It is wise to cook only 1 portion at once.

Heat the butter gently until it turns a golden colour and crack the eggs into the pan. Cook the eggs carefully, as you like them. Season and slide onto a warm plate.

Pour 2 tablespoons of Vinegar into the pan, reduce by half and add the tomato and parsley and coat the eggs.

Clean out the pan with kitchen paper and repeat the process.

Garnish with flat leaf parsley.

"The college lecturer had never had anyone question his method of presentation. This was only the beginning — who was missing the point, him or me? **JBS**

CHEEKY LOBSTER FOR SUMMER
Serves Two

Ingredients:

1lb/450g Fresh Cooked Lobster
4 pieces Cooked Asparagus
2 wedges Seasonal Melon
Fresh Dill
¼pt White Wine
1oz/25g Butter
1oz/25g Finely Chopped Onion
Nasturtium Leaves and Flowers
Assorted Lettuce Leaves

Method:

Using a sharp knife, cut the cooked lobster in half on a flat chopping board, have a cloth on hand to wipe away any juice or water discharged.
Crack the lobster claws open and remove the meat (use a kitchen hammer if possible, or try nut crackers).

Warm a large frying pan and add the butter and onion and keep on a low light. Add the lobster tail meat from each side of the shell (discard any dark or green areas). Gently cook claws and tail, add the cooked asparagus and a sprinkle of white wine and fresh dill, simmer for two minutes.

Arrange the lettuce leaves on to your plate, spoon on the lobster and asparagus.

Wipe the nasturtium leaves gently around the warm pan with melon wedges and arrange around the lobster.

Garnish of fresh mint and lime if you so wish, the choice is yours.

Appears in "The Summer Delights" Recipe Book.

"Our new German Head Chef wore wooden clogs on his first day. He'd never worn them before, you could tell. He tripped up on many occasions and kept falling over in them. I chuckled, but stopped when he carved a chefs hat out of a potato. I bought clogs myself the next week"
John Benson Smith 1979

VINAIGRETTE
Makes ¼ Pint/150ml

Ingredients:

1 tbsp   Champagne Vinegar
1 tbsp   Red Wine
1 tbsp   Dijon Mustard
6-8 tbsp   Peanut Oil
          Sea Salt
          Freshly Ground Black Pepper

Method:

Combine all the ingredients, except the Peanut oil, add this last.
Season to taste.

Cookery is taken from one extreme to another, from camp-fire cooking to the highest standards of haute cuisine and cuisine perfection.

The first impression of the meal is always the most important for a customer. Starting the meal off on the right footing can transform the simplest delicacies into the most intricate specialities. An Hors D'oeuvre should be light and delicate and should be served in small quantities to tantalise the appetite for the meal to follow.

As a larder chef I like to think of my role as similar to that of a chemist, on receiving a prescription, making up recipes and dishes using formulas and proportions to conceive a perfect product. This enables the customer to be able to appreciate the highest standards of Haute Cuisine.

Each and every person has different preferences, dislikes and unfortunately allergies, or special diets which affect their daily food intake. This makes the role of the chef an extremely important one, a job which must be done with absolute precision.

MATTHEW BENSON SMITH

"If you want to be a chef, try and do it well every day, and get better and better — if not, drive a bus or work in an estate agents or solicitors — it isn't worth it"   **JBS**

ABOUT JOHN BENSON SMITH
"Something of a pioneer when it comes to cooking up the Best of British food — no foreign fancy food — just delicate and full of flavour and a revelation to those who thought the British culinary heritage was stodgy, bland and boring"
James Chapman, Yorkshire Evening Press

TO COMMENCE

TIPS:
— Season Red Meats after cooking, not before, as it draws the blood.
— Boiled Eggs with shell on won't spin in one place, a raw one will.
— Place a drop of vinegar into cooked potatoes to stop then from overcooking in water.
— Cubes of clean sponge dipped in warm water and vinegar removes finger marks and dribbles from plate rims.
— Leave baby onions in olive oil overnight, skins are then easily removed.
— Keep raw meats prior to cooking away from heat.
— Milk rapidly boiling over? Place cold spoon or ladle into the pan to stop it.

SOUPS

CHILLED AVOCADO AND WATERCRESS SOUP
Serves Six

Ingredients:

2	Avocados (ripe, skin and stone removed)
2 bunches	Watercress (thoroughly washed)
2½pts/1k 500g	Cold Strong Chicken Stock
	Juice of one Lemon
½pt/300ml	Double Cream

Method:

Place all the ingredients together in the blender (except the cream), saving the chives for a garnish.

Strain the cold soup through a fine sieve and add the cream, correct the seasoning. Refrigerate.

Garnish with chopped chives on top of each bowl.

A little Salt and Pepper to taste. Some fresh chives to garnish.

"My first recollection of soups was my father's potato soup which he burnt on the Aga — a week later he melted the bottom out of the kettle"
John Benson Smith

CHILLED MINT AND CUCUMBER SOUP
Serves Four

Chill the Soup Tureen or Bowl in advance in the freezer.
Often one's palate is easier to please and taste with cold foods, as opposed to hot.

Ingredients:

        Fresh Mint to taste
1 tsp Mint Sauce
½ pt Double Cream
1½ pt Cold Chicken Stock
½ Cucumber (Chopped)
        Lemon Juice from ½ lemon
        Seasoning

Method:

Prepare a chicken stock which needs to be strained, skimmed and cooled.

Place in a liquidiser the fresh mint and cucumber pieces and lemon juice. Liquidise until a purée.
Add the chicken stock, a teaspoon of mint sauce and blend. Finish with the cream. Taste and season.

Blend again a little and pour into chilled bowls.

Garnish with chopped mint.
Serve.

WARM CREAM OF FLOWER SOUP
Serves Four

A taste difficult to describe …
Note: See Cooking with Flowers

Ingredients:

1¾pt/1 ltr Milk/Cream
2oz Cornflour (and Elderflower Cordial to consistency)
        Seasoning
10 tbsp Mixed Flowers (not sprayed or chemicalised) eg. marigolds, pinks, carnations, nasturtiums, roses, etc.

Method:

Bring the milk to the boil. Dissolve the cornflour in the elderflower cordial and use to bind the boiling milk. Keep warm. Add the washed flower petals and infuse for one hour on a warm plate. Pass through a strainer, liquidise the pulp and return to the soup. Season as you wish, eg. salt, pepper, lemon juice, etc.

Garnish with flower petals.
Serve warm.

"Michael Quinn was always my real hero. He took down so many barriers and paved a way for others to follow, he was interested in your life and families and not just gaining press guide and magazine articles, A carrot was a carrot and didn't need messing with!"
John Benson Smith

"College was always like having toothache — it only stopped when you passed the exam. My home economics teacher at school in my report said, "this boy shows no interest whatsoever in this subject and cannot retain any information at all". Maybe she was right"
John Benson Smith

CREAM OF ASPARAGUS SOUP
Serves Six

Ingredients:

    4oz/100g Butter
    4oz/100g Flour
4¼ pt/3½ ltr Chicken Stock
   2lb/900g   Asparagus Stalks
7fl.oz/175ml Cream

Method:

With the butter and flour prepare a blond roux letting it cool slightly.

Strain and skim the chicken stock and while still boiling mix into the roux gradually.

Cut the asparagus stalks into pieces, blanch, drain and add to the soup.

Bring soup to the boil, skim and season then simmer gently for 45 minutes. Pass through a fine strainer into a clean pan and reboil and skim.

Add the cream to the soup and correct the consistency and seasoning.

Garnish with asparagus heads.

MARIGOLD SOUP
Serves Four

Note: See Cooking with Flowers

Ingredients:

  1 tbsp Flour
8oz/225g Potatoes
 1 Large Onion (diced small)
  2 tbsp Celery (chopped)
  6 tbsp Marigold Petals (chopped)
  2 tbsp Oil
1pt/600ml Water
1pt/600ml Milk
          Seasoning
  2 tbsp Fresh Parsley

Method:

Chop the peeled onions very small and fry in oil in a large pan, add the peeled potatoes, chopped into small squares, the celery and one tablespoon of parsley.

Leave to fry for 1 minute then add enough water to just cover the vegetables. Leave to cook for 20 minutes over a low fire. Do not stir or it will mash the cubes of potato.

Keep half of milk back and add the rest of the milk to the vegetables. Mix remaining milk and flour to a smooth paste and add to Soup.

Bring to the boil whist stirring carefully, add the Marigold petals and season.

Keep stirring until Soup thickens. Sprinkle the remaining parsley on top and serve.

Garnish with a few flower petals and whipped cream.

MATTHEW BENSON SMITH

French Experience: 4 weeks; École Le Notre, Paris.

Thoughts on France: *"Overall the month was a superb experience. Learning the different cooking styles and techniques from the highly skilled and respected Chef Monsieur Tash helped to strengthen my ability and strive for higher more educated and inspired standards. I covered a lot of ground including hot kitchen work, cold buffet work, Crustaceouse and fish. France conjours many fond memories."*

"An imaginative and interesting menu offers some delightful dishes which are cooked to a high standard with impressive sauces and first rate presentation"
Egon Ronay

CHILLED EXOTIC FRUIT SOUP
Serves Four

Served as a Sweet also

Ingredients:

1	Small Mango
2	Kiwi Fruit
2	Passion Fruit
20	Strawberries
16	Raspberries (fresh)
1 tbsp	Chopped Fresh Mint
½ pt	Cream

Syrup:

6 tbsp	Sugar
1	Mint Sprig
1	Clove
¼ tsp	Mixed Chinese Spices
	Thinly sliced zest of 1 Lime
	Thinly sliced zest of ¼ Lemon
¼	Vanilla Pod (split lengthways)
½ tsp	Finely chopped Root Ginger
2	Coriander Seeds
1 pt	Water

Method:

To make the syrup: in a thick bottomed pan combine sugar, mint, clove, spices, zests, ginger, vanilla pod, coriander and ¾ pint of water, and boil.

Keep stirring until sugar dissolves. Simmer 10 mins. Remove from heat and infuse.

Meanwhile peel the mango and cut the flesh into pieces the same size.
Wash the strawberries, peel the kiwi and cut and prepare the fruits as you require. Scoop out the passion fruit.

When the syrup is cool, strain and add to the fruits. Add the cream. Chill for 2 hours.

Serve and garnish as you wish.

PAUL BOCUSE SOUPE AUX TRUFFLES ELYSEES
Serves One

This dish was created by Paul Bocuse for President and Mme. Valery Giscard d'Estaing and served at a Luncheon given at the Elysee Palace.

A sensational Consommé sealed in Puff Pastry.

Ingredients:

2oz	Diced Carrot, Celery and Mushroom
¼oz/50g	Black Truffle, thinly sliced (tinned or fresh)
1oz/20g	Pâté de Foie Gras, diced (tinned or fresh)
8fl.oz/225ml	Chicken Consommé
3-4oz/50-75g	Puff Pastry
	Egg Wash (1 egg, 1 yoke, pinch sugar and salt, mix well)
	Seasoning

Method:

Combine the diced vegetables, truffle, foie gras and consommé in an individual heat-proof porcelain soup bowl.
Cut out piece of puff pastry.

Brush the edges of a round of puff pastry, large enough to fit over the soup bowl, allowing for an overlap of ¾" all round.
Using the egg wash, seal the side down and crimp to a pattern.
Chill for 20 minutes.
Decorate the top with a pattern if required.

Brush the top of the pastry round with egg yolk and bake in the middle of a preheated oven for 15 minutes or until pastry is well coloured golden brown on Gas Mark 6 (200°C, 400°F).

Serve immediately.

ABOUT JOHN BENSON SMITH
"Regional specialities are imaginatively presented in modern style and served with calm confidence that comes with love for and deep knowledge of the subject"
Joan Poulson "Food in Yorkshire"

AS APPRENTICE:
"I wore a shirt, tie and jumper under my chefs jacket on the first day, but I was scared, I couldn't get my chefs checks over my jeans! The Sous Chef said it was a good job I hadn't come to work on a motorcycle"
JBS

TO CONTINUE

FISH

FISH

ROULADE OF LEMON SOLE AND SALMON

COULIBIAC OF SALMON

FILLET OF LEMON SOLE LAWRENCE

SEA BASS WITH SEAWEED

FILEY COBLE STEW

FILLET OF PLAICE WITH CABBAGE

FISHERMAN'S CATCH

ROAST MONKFISH

TURBOT

MILLE FEUILLE DE SAUMON AU CHERVIL

ROULADE OF LEMON SOLE AND SALMON
Serves Four

Ingredients:

1 lb	Fresh Lemon Sole Fillet (skinned)	
1 lb	Fresh Salmon Fillet (sliced and skinned)	
2/4	Fresh Leaf Spinach Leaves (washed)	

Mousse:

½ lb	Plaice Fillets (skinned)
2	Egg Whites
4fl.oz	Double Cream
1/2 bunch	Fresh Watercress
	Seasoning

Method:

Chop up the plaice fillet and season. Liquidise in a food processor, then purée with the watercress and egg white slowly until creamy consistency. Pass with a fine sieve with the aid of a plastic scraper, mix with the cream and refrigerate.

Lightly flatten the lemon sole fillets to form a sheet. Do this also to the salmon. Blanche and re-fresh the whole spinach leaves, lay them flat and refrigerate also. Lay the salmon onto tin foil, then the sole then the spinach. Spread the mousse to the centre and gently roll up the tin foil. Bake the roulade, wrapped in the foil at a low to moderate temperature, for approximately 20-30 mins., or until the centre is hot. Un-roll and serve in three 2 inch portions.

TIPS:
— A little black pepper sprinkled on a hot stove top will clear the kitchen of unwanted guests.
— Sprinkle hot pan handles with flour to warn others of danger.
— Scale fresh fish inside a large plastic bag.
— Rub fruits with a little olive oil for displays.

COULIBIAC OF SALMON

Serves Two

A modern interpretation of a 'classic', a Signature Dish of our Restaurant portraying a typical example of our Fayre.

Ingredients:

11oz/300g	Salmon (filleted, skinned and boned)
1	Egg (boiled and sliced)
2oz/50g	Melted Butter
1oz/25g	Buckwheat (cooked)
	Seasoning
1oz/25g	Strips of Vegetables
4oz/100g	Puff Pastry
1 measure	White Wine
	Juice of 1 Lemon
	Zest of ¼ Lime
6fl.oz/150ml	Double Cream
6fl.oz/150ml	Fish Stock

Method:

Butter a 3″ bowl and line with the pastry, moulding to shape.

With a cutter, cut a circle of Salmon and cut horizontally to form 2 pieces. Place one into the bowl, place on top the boiled egg, buckwheat, vegetables and season. Place on top the other slice of Salmon and season again. Cover with pastry lid, seal and brush with egg yolk and make a hole in the centre.

Place on a baking sheet and bake for approximately 12-15 minutes at 150°C. Half way through cooking time pour the melted butter through the hole in the pastry, while the Coulibiac continues to cook.

Reduce a small amount of fish stock by half with White Wine and lime juice, then add double cream with lime zest. Season and reduce to thicken.

Remove the Coulibiac from the oven, cut around carefully with a knife and turn out. Egg yolk quickly and place in a hot oven to colour.

Pour sauce onto base of plate. Place Coulibiac onto the sauce and decorate with three small garnishes of German, Red and Black Caviars and fresh herb. Serve.

FILLET OF LEMON SOLE LAWRENCE

Serves Four

Dedicated to 'The Kitchen Porter', here and everywhere. As important as anyone, if not more so!!

Ingredients:

4	Fresh Lemon Sole Fillets (skinned)
4	Large Spinnach Leaves (blanched)
4oz	Fresh Crab Meat

Butter Sauce:

2 tsp	White Wine
2 tsp	Champagne Vinegar
¼lb	Chopped Butter
	Seasoning
4oz	Chopped Mixed Peppers and Onion
	Splash of Cream (whipping)

Method:

Line the individual non-stick pudding tin with with the lightly cooked spinach, then line over this the fish fillet neatly. Fill the middle with crab meat and lightly compact. Poach or steam in the tin and cook lightly. Allow to cool for one minute, turn out in the centre of the plate.

Reduce the wine and vinegar by half. Stir in the butter until dissolved. Add the peppers, onions, splash of cream and season.

Coat with the butter sauce, and serve.

ABOUT JOHN BENSON SMITH
"Chef de Cuisine at the famous Black Swan, Helmsley, Gold Medal holder and named as one of Britains top up and coming chefs"
John Highfield, Sheffield Star

SEA BASS WITH SEAWEED
Serves Two

Ingredients:

16oz/450g (approx) Sea Bass (filleted,
              skinned and boned)
              Seasoning
              Herbs
4oz/100g Pastry
              Egg Wash (1 egg and 1 yolk)
4fl.oz/100ml Provençal Sauce
              Seaweed (tinned)

Provencal Sauce:

½oz/10g Butter
¾oz/15g Finely chopped Shallots
3g Garlic
1 tsp Tomato Puree
4fl.oz/100ml Stock
1oz/25g Tomato Concasse
            Seasoning

Method:

Season the fillets of Sea Bass and place
fresh herbs on the top.

Wrap in lattice cut pastry and brush lightly
with egg wash.

Bake in oven at 150°C for approximately
10 minutes.

Sauce:

Gently sweat shallots in butter. Add garlic
and tomato purée. Add stock and finish
with tomato concasse and seasoning.

To Finish:

Cover the plate with Provençal Sauce.
Place the Sea Bass in centre and arrange
seaweed around Sea Bass. Serve.

FILEY COBLE STEW
Serves Six

Ingredients:

1lb/450g Prawns
1½-2lb/675-900g Crab
¾pt/450ml Bechamel (fairly thin)
2 heaped tbsp Lancashire Cheese
              (grated)
2 Egg Yolks
2 tsp Double Cream
3oz/75g Butter
4oz/100g Mushrooms (chopped)
1 small clove Garlic (chopped)
2lb/900g Creamed Potatoes
              Salt and Pepper

Method:

Remove all the shellfish from the shells.
Place all the shells in a pan and add the
Bechamel Sauce. Simmer for 15 minutes.
Pass through a fine strainer.
Add cream, egg yolks and cheese, stirring
until thick. Do not reboil.
Season and add half the butter.

Cook the mushrooms and garlic in the
remaining butter. Add to the sauce with the
shellfish meat. Season and place into a pie
dish, top with the creamed potato.

Garnish with shellfish and watercress.

FILLET OF PLAICE WITH CABBAGE
Serves Four

A Personal Favourite

Ingredients:

12oz/300g	Approx. Plaice (filleted, skinned and boned)
4oz/100g	Cabbage
1oz/25g	Shallots
	Seasoning
1 measure	White Wine
4fl.oz/100ml	Double Cream
2fl.oz/50ml	Fish Stock
	Caviar
	Mint Leaves
½oz/10g	Butter

Mousse:

1	Egg White
4oz/100g	Salmon
1oz/25g	Leeks
	Seasoning
1 fl.oz/25ml	Double Cream

Method:

Chop salmon and leeks, purée. Add egg whites, cream and seasoning.

Roll Salmon and Leek Mousse in Plaice fillets and season.

Sweat the shallots in butter, add white wine and fish stock. Poach the Plaice in liquor at 80°C for approximately 5-10 minutes. Blanch the chiffonard of cabbage and arrange in the centre of the plate.

Remove the Plaice from stock when cooked and place on the centre of the cabbage. Reduce stock down and finish with cream, seasoning and butter (monte au buerre).

Nape sauce over Plaice and make an insertion in the top. Garnish with caviar and mint leaves.
Serve.

"We decided to stay for Sunday night. Thank goodness we did. Otherwise we would never have discovered the delights of the Black Swan's kitchen when it extends itself. It is not cheap, but the menu and wine list are better than most in rural France. The meal for two cost us just over £50 — and we did push out the boat with the Vosné Romanée."
Bill Condie, Weekend Telegraph

Fillet of Plaice with Cabbage

FISHERMAN'S CATCH
Serves Four

Including Salmon, Turbot, Monkfish, Prawns and Crayfish, tossed in Butter and White Wine

Fisherman's Catch

Ingredients:

1lb 8oz	Assorted Fish (prepared, skinned and cut into 1″ cubes)
4oz/100g	Vegetables (cut into fine strips)
10g	Asparagus (chopped)
200ml	White Wine
200ml	Fish Stock
100ml	Cream
8oz/200g	Puff Pastry (rolled thinly, cut into trellis, cooked over a glass bowl)
4oz/100g	Butter
	Seasoning
4 small	Crayfish
1 bunch	Parsley

Method:

Gently sweat the vegetables with the fish and the white wine and cook gently, remove the fish after 3-4 minutes, add the fish stock. Reduce by half.

Add the cream and gently add the 4oz butter.

Replace the fish into the sauce. Season well (do not re-boil).

Put the fish and sauce in the centre of each plate. Garnish with a crayfish and a sprig of parsley and top with a net of puff pastry.

"Chefs cannot produce miracles with mountains, loaves and fishes ... only sometimes"
John Benson Smith

ROAST MONKFISH
With Garlic and a Chive Butter Sauce

A cheap fish until healthy foods came along

Ingredients:

1lb 8oz/750g	Trimmed Monkfish Tail
2.8oz/75g	Chopped Vegetables
2 cloves	Crushed Garlic
2oz/50g	Butter
4oz/100g	Small Pearls of Vegetables
6 fl.oz	White Wine Vinegar/ White Wine
125-150g	Butter
1 Bunch	Chives (chopped)

Method:

Seal in a hot tray with a little butter the chopped vegetables and monkfish, cover and place in a moderate oven for 10-15 minutes.

In the tray used for cooking, reduce the white wine and vinegar by half. Remove from the heat.

Gently whisk in the 125g of butter. Strain and add the pearls of vegetables (do not re-boil).

Remove the monkfish from the oven, slice lengthways into medallions, place each portion in a circle in the centre of each plate, coat with the butter sauce and sprinkle with chopped chives.

Garnish with criss cross of mange tout and tomato flesh.
Serve.

"If you ever get the chance to see a monkfish's head — don't!!"

TURBOT
Poached in Champagne with Spinach Mousse and Cream

"The sight in La Napoule of fresh fish being delivered to restaurant L'Oasis, turbots still flinching, was amazing"

Ingredients:

1lb 8oz	Turbot (4 pieces, skinned, prepared)
50g	Butter
25g	Shallots (chopped)
200ml	Champagne
200ml	Fish Stock
100ml	Cream
1oz	Truffle
	Chopped Parsley
1 pinch	Saffron

Fish Mousse

12oz	Fish
1	Egg
100ml	Cream
	Seasoning
3 leaves	Fresh Spinach (washed)

Method: (Fish Mousse)

Chop the fish and spinach in a food processor with the egg until very smooth

Gently add the cream and season well.

Butter 4 small moulds, add the mousse and cook in a Bain Marie in a moderate oven.

Method:

Sweat the shallots in a little butter, add the turbot pieces, the champagne and fish stock and poach gently for 10-15 minutes. Remove turbot and keep warm.

Reduce the cooking liquor and add the cream.

Season well, add a little saffron and whisk in a little butter (do not re-boil).

Place the turbot portions on the 4 plates, turn out the four mousses onto the top of each plate, strain the sauce through a fine chimoir over each portion.

Garnish with a slice of truffle and a little chopped parsley.

"You also deal with God and nature, weather and seasons, things grow and move prior to preparation for the table"
John Benson Smith

Turbot

MILLE FEUILLE DE SAUMON AU CHERVIL
(Thin layers of puff pastry with salmon and chervil)
Serves Four

In the style of Louis Outhier

Ingredients:

12oz/350g	Puff Pastry rolled into a 17 x 14 inch (42.5 x 35cm) rectangle
1 tsp/5ml	Unsalted Butter
1 tsp/5ml	Finely chopped Shallots
¼ pt/100ml	Dry White Wine
½ pt/225ml	Double Cream
1 lb/450g	Fresh Scotch Salmon, very thinly sliced, no bones
2 tsp/10ml	Finely chopped Chervil Seasoning

Method:

Roll out pastry thinly. Roll out salmon.
Prick the rolled out Puff Pastry with a fork and place on a baking tray 17 x 14 inch (42.5 x 35cm) which has been lightly brushed with water. Cover the tray with a wire rack to stop it rising. Bake in the oven on Gas Mark 6 for 15 minutes, then reduce the temperature to Gas Mark 4 (180°C, 350°F) and cook for further minutes. Remove and keep warm.

In a small saucepan add the butter and the shallots, cook gently and slowly but don't colour, add the wine and reduce by half, add the cream, boil until it thickens, season and keep warm.

Using a serrated long sharp knife cut the cooled pastry into four equal rectangles and keep warm. In a large hot non-stick clean frying pan seal the salmon slices on each side for a few moments until just cooked. Layer the pastry and salmon alternately starting and concluding with the pastry. Trim mille feuille and divide.

Place on hot plates, pour over and around the sauce, garnish with the chervil and serve.

"We discovered that the Black Swan does not serve average pub grub. Cold meats, salads of leaves normally found only in Provence, and the best part of a side of smoked salmon duly arrived with half a bottle of very respectable champagne bearing the hotel's own label. Our spirits rose." **Bill Condie, Weekend Telegraph**

TO CONTINUE

MAIN COURSES

STRIPS OF CHICKEN BREAST WITH CHIVES AND
ENGLISH WHITE WINE

ROASTING CHICKEN IN SEA SALT

WILD DUCK WITH MANDARINS

JUGGED HARE

DOMES OF HAM AND CUCUMBER

RUMP STEAK AND POTATO PUDDING

VENISON WITH BILBERRIES

BEEF GOWERDALE

FILLET OF LAMB WITH PORT AND COURGETTE

ROAST FILLET OF BEEF WITH BUTTER SAUCE

SUPREME OF CHICKEN INDONESIENNE

LOBSTER SALAD WITH AVOCADO

LES SUPREMES DE VOLAILLE TROIS COULEURS

"I have not tried to teach mother how to suck eggs with a lot of basic and apparent straightforward roast main courses (my favourite with green peas and crispy roast potatoes), but my respect is paramount to a chef and kitchen that can do this task well, vast amounts cannot, it is equal to modern pretty bits and bobs on plates, if not more so. It is not a case of who killed off Cock Robin, but who killed off roast chicken and real peas, far more use to us all than either the Black Forest gateaux brigade and the scallops with yogurt, basic sorbet and kiwi fruit gang"
John Benson Smith

TIPS:
— Place oranges in the freezer for ½ hour to ease slicing.
— Parsley keeps well in the fridge sprinkled with water, in a plastic bag.
— Rest cooked Lamb for 20 minutes prior to carving.
— The heavier the Grapefruit, the larger the juice content.
— To remove skin from flat wet fish, dry your hands with salt.

MAIN COURSE

STRIPS OF CHICKEN BREAST WITH CHIVES AND ENGLISH WHITE WINE
Serves Two

Dedicated to a chef who influenced me greatly

Ingredients:

2oz/50g	Butter
½ bunch	Chives (washed and chopped)
1pt/600ml	Double Cream
one-eighth	Chicken Stock
	Seasoning
2	Watercress Leaves
2	Tomatoes (red and firm)
2 measures	English White Wine (Lamberhurst)
2 x 7oz/2 x 215g	Fresh Chicken Breast
¼	Lime
	Seasoned Flour

Method:

Trim and smarten the Chicken Breast. Cut into five strips, lightly flour and cook gently in the butter (no colour) on a low heat. Remove when half cooked. Place in a little cream in a dish and continue to cook under the grill slowly.

In a pan reduce the Lamberhurst by half, add the chicken stock, reduce, add the cream and reduce. Season and add lime juice, reduce to thicken.
Return the chicken strips to the pan and simmer.

Remove with a sharp knife, in one piece from top to bottom, the skin from the tomato and curl to form a rose.
Sprinkle the chives onto the chicken and sauce. Add a little of the grilling cream and reduce, stir in a little butter.
Serve on a plate.

Try to form the strips into a log criss-crossed effect. **Garnish** with the tomato rose and watercress leaf.

"I shall never be happy unless one of my brigade, past or present, really makes it to the top and becomes a household name and carves a notch in the world of food"
John Benson Smith

ROASTING CHICKEN IN SEA SALT
Serves Four

Use either method A or B

Ingredients:

3lb/1k 150g Fresh Chicken
6lb/2k 300g Coarse Salt/Sea Salt

Method A:

Prepare the chicken for the oven.
Remove the giblets, season with black
pepper, sprinkle with fresh garden herbs
inside and smear the skin with a little wild
garlic.

Line the roasting tray or pan with foil. Coat
the bottom with a layer of salt.
Place the chicken in the centre and cover
with salt. Place in the oven at Gas Mark 7
(230°C, 430°F) for 2 hours.
Remove from the oven.
Break the salt to remove, and serve the
chicken.

Retain the salt for another time.
Its flavour, scent and texture is
incomparable.

SALT PASTRY

Ingredients:

2½lb/1kg Strong White Flour
1lb 5oz/600g Fine Table Salt
7 Egg Whites
Egg Wash (2 yolks, milk and
caster sugar)
Water to correct texture

Method B:

Combine flour and salt in a mixer at low
speed for 1-2 minutes. Add the egg whites
and increase to medium speed. Add the
cold water slowly. Roll out around the
chicken forming a chicken shape and bake
for 40 minutes approximately.

Note:

Brush with melted butter before leaving
kitchen.

WILD DUCK WITH MANDARINS
Serves Four

Wild Duck a scurge to many, a joy to others

Ingredients:

1 large Mallard Duck
Bouquet Garni
4oz/100g Cooked Noodles
1 Onion
1 level dspn Fresh chopped Parsley
½ level tsp Thyme
Pinch Nutmeg
4 dspn Honey
2 dspn Beer
2 Egg Yolks
2½fl.oz/62g Double Cream
3 Mandarin Oranges
2fl.oz/50g Port
Lemon Juice
Salt and Black Pepper

Garnish:

Mandarin Oranges and Watercress

Method:

Clean the duck giblets and put them in a
saucepan with water to cover; add salt,
freshly ground black pepper and the
bouquet garni. Cover the pan with a lid
and cook for about 25 minutes or until the
giblets are tender. Strain and set the
cooking liquid aside. Skin the gizzard and
chop this, the heart and liver finely.

Chop the drained noodles roughly and mix
in the giblets, chopped onion, herbs and
nutmeg. Mix half the honey and half the
beer with the egg yolks and cream and stir
this into the noodle mixture. Open the vent
and remove any knobs of fat from the
duck, spoon in the stuffing and close the
opening.

Put the duck in a roasting tin, breast
downwards and pour water in the pan to a
depth of ½ inch. Roast in the centre of a
preheated oven at Gas Mark 5 (375°F) for
20 minutes, basting occasionally. Remove
the duck from the roasting pan, put in a
wire rack and replace the duck, breast
upwards. Pour the remaining honey and
beer over the duck and continue roasting
for a further 30 minutes, or until the duck
is crisp and golden and the legs are tender
when tested with a skewer.

Meanwhile grate the rind from the
mandarin oranges and set aside. Having
first removed the pith and pips, put the
fruit in the liquidiser.

When the duck is ready, lift it on to a
warm serving dish. Add the mandarin pulp
and rind to the pan, together with the port
and ½ pint of the reserved giblet stock.
Boil on top of the stove over a high heat
until the gravy has reduced and thickened
slightly. Sharpen with lemon juice and
adjust seasoning. Strain the gravy into a
warm sauce boat.

Garnish the duck with watercress sprigs
and thin slices of unpeeled mandarin.
Serve with roast or duchess potatoes and
buttered green beans.

TRADITIONAL JUGGED HARE
Serves Six

Ingredients:

1	Hare (fresh)
½lb/225g	Button Mushrooms (3 per person)
½lb/225g	Lean Bacon
½ bottle	Red Wine
1lb/450g	Button Onions (3 per person)
2oz/50g	Butter
2oz/50g	Dripping
1oz/25g	Flour
	Hares blood from preparation
⅓ Gill	Cream
Bunch	Herbs
1 clove	Garlic
1 tsp	Tomato Puree

Preparation:

Preparation of hare for jugged hare must be done on the day before it is to be served.

Cut off legs at first joint.
Place the hare on the chopping board on its back. Make a slit with the point of a small knife in the hind leg lengthwise to enable a finger to be inserted, ensure that only the skin is cut, this can be achieved by raising the skin from the flesh.
Break down the connective tissue between the skin and the flesh.
Remove the skin from the legs, then continue to draw the skin off up to the ears; these should be cut off close to the bone. Remove the skin entirely from the head, cutting the last part of the skin at the mouth.
Make an incision in the middle of the belly to open it up from the legs to the ribs. Cut open the middle part separating the two legs to remove the intestines. Take out the intestines and place in a basin. Pour out the blood which will be used in preparing the jugged hare, add a little vinegar so that it retains its fluid state. Remove liver, lungs and heart, retain liver.
Cut hare into serving pieces, ie 2 legs, 3-5 pieces of back and forelegs.
Soak the pieces overnight in ½ bottle of red wine, 2 measures of brandy and fresh herbs.

Method:

Heat dripping and brown pieces of hare then sprinkle with the flour. Add the red wine in which the hare has soaked and mix well.
Add sufficient water or brown stock to cover, the tomato puree, crushed clove of garlic, salt, pepper and the herbs. Cover and cook in the oven at 325°F for 1 hour.

Brown onions in a pan with butter.
Add the onions, diced bacon and mushrooms.
Return to the oven and cook for a further 1 to 2 hours.
Mix the hares blood with a few spoonfuls of the sauce and the cream, return to the sauce.
Bring back to the boil, remove the herbs and keep hot (not boiling).

Garnish with hare shaped fried bread slices dipped at one end in chopped parsley and the other end in redcurrant jelly.

DOMES OF HAM AND CUCUMBER
Serves Six
Cut to use — lean cooked gammon

Ingredients:

12oz/350g	Puff Pastry
4oz/100g	Butter (plus a little extra for greasing)
5oz/150g	Mushrooms (chopped into ½"/1cm pieces)
1 large	Onion (cut into ½"/1cm dice)
1½lb/450g	Lean Cooked Gammon
2oz/50g	Plain Flour (sifted)
½pt/300ml	Chicken Stock
½pt/300ml	Double Cream
Pinch	Fennel Seeds
Bunch	Chives (finely chopped)
1oz/25g	Parsley (finely chopped)
1	Cucumber (cut into ½"/1cm dice)
2oz/50g	Spinnach (cooked and chopped)
	Salt and Freshly Ground Black Pepper
	Lemon Juice
	Ground Nutmeg
1 clove	Garlic (crushed)
	Egg yolk for glazing

Method:

Roll out the puff pastry thinly and cut out from it 6 shapes to fit the inside of 6 round 3 inch/7.5cm Pyrex overproof dishes, and 6 circles to form lids. Place these in the refrigerator to chill for 10 minutes or so. Grease the dishes themselves.
Meanwhile melt the butter in a saucepan and add the mushrooms, onion and gammon. Cook until the vegetables are tender. Remove from heat, mix in the flour, cover with a lid and place in a hot oven Gas Mark 7 (220°C, 425°F) for 3 minutes. Remove, cool slightly then gradually incorporate the chicken stock and double cream. Return to the boil, add the fennel seeds, chives, parsley, cucumber and spinach and simmer over a gentle heat for 15 minutes. Season to taste and leave until cool.

Line the Pyrex moulds with the puff pastry. Half fill them with the gammon mixture, reserve any excess. Brush the inside of the pastry lids with egg yolk and place them on top of the domes. Crimp them around the edge to form a seal. Bake the domes in a hot oven Gas Mark 8 (230°C, 450°F) for 10-15 minutes. Remove, leave to cool slightly, then with the help of a small knife, free each pastry dome from its dish and turn them upside down on a baking tray. Brush with egg yolk again and return to the oven for a further 5 minutes to colour the pastry golden brown.

Cover the base of 6 serving plates with any excess gammon sauce, reheated, and carefully place a dome in the centre of each. Decorate with chopped fresh herbs and sliced red pepper, and Serve.
Garnish with chopped fresh herbs and thinly sliced red pepper.

RUMP STEAK AND POTATO PUDDING
Serves Four

Ingredients:

1lb/450g	Rump Steak (tender, fatless and no sinew) ½ inch cube
¾lb/350g	Suet Paste
¼lb/100g	New Cooked Potatoes
1pt/600ml	Beef Gravy
2oz/50g	Onion Seasoning

Method:

Butter and line 4 individual pudding basins with the soft paste, seal off the meat, potato and onion in a hot pan and place into the centre of the puddings and season. Cover with gravy. Lay a circular piece of paste over the top. Moisten, fold and seal. Steam for 1 hour, cool slightly and turn out onto hot plate, coat with a little extra sauce and serve.
Garnish with a little watercress or fresh mint.

VENISON WITH BILBERRIES
Serves Four

Ingredients:

12	Noisettes cut from a saddle of Venison
1oz/25g	Butter
½pt/300ml	Vinaigrette (seasoned with plenty of freshly ground black pepper)
2 tbsp	Double Cream
4oz/100g	Bilberries
1½ tbsp	Bilberry Jelly
	Salt and Pepper
2 tbsp	Cognac

Marinade:

1pt/600ml	Olive Oil
¼pt/150ml	Vinegar
	Peppercorns
	Parsley
	Thyme
	Bay Leaf

Garnish:

2	Pears (peeled and halved)
2oz/50g	Butter
12	Chestnuts (peeled and boiled until tender)

Method:

Mix the ingredients for the marinade and pour over the venison. Leave for 2-3 hours, turning occasionally. Dry the venison and fry in the butter. Keep the meat warm while you prepare the sauce: deglaze the pan with the vinaigrette and reduce by half.

In a separate pan, slightly reduce the cream with the bilberries. Stir this mixture into the reduced vinaigrette, add the bilberry jelly, bring to the boil and check the seasoning. Stir in the Cognac.

For the Garnish:

Fry the pear halves gently in 1oz of the butter until golden. Slice vertically in a fan shape. Fry the chestnuts in the remaining butter.

To Serve:

Divide the bilberry sauce between four plates and arrange the venison on top. Garnish with the glazed pear and glazed chestnuts.

JOHN BENSON SMITH

French Experience: L'Oasis Restaurant La Napoule

Thoughts on France: *"An intriguing and opportune time spent working in one of the world's finest restaurants shrouded with accolades and awards. No doubt Louis Outhier's style of cuisine will have influenced me in my approach to rewarding English food with its true identity. The romantic food styles of the french signify to me the true magic of France. Let us take to the kitchens while we are young and leave playing cricket until we are older."*

"A unique style of foods formed from our History and Heritage. A proud collection of interesting and intriguing recipes greeted us on our studies and research: no longer will we 'The British Chefs' be quietened by our overseas counterparts.
The time has come at last for us to firmly stamp our mark on the map of the world —
Yorkshireman — British and proud of it — Britain in Bloom"

John Benson Smith

Beef Gowerdale

BEEF GOWERDALE
Serves Four

Modern interpretation of Beef Wellington

Ingredients:

4 x 8oz	Fillet Steaks (trimmed)
8oz	Puff Pastry (rolled thinly, cut into trellis)
4oz	Pâté (Chicken Liver or Goose)
4oz	Duxelle of Mushrooms (chopped onion and mushrooms)
150ml	Madeira
25g	Shallot
	Stuffed Courgette (with carrot)
50g	Butter
150ml	Demiglaze (thickend Veal Stock)
1	Egg Yolk

Method:

Seal off the steaks in a hot pan, make a pocket in the middle of each, stuff with Pâté.

Top the steak with the mushroom mixture and encase with pastry and egg yolk with a brush.

Cook in a medium to hot oven for 15 to 20 minutes depending on required degree of cooking.

Sweat shallots in a saute pan and add the Madeira. Reduce by half, add the demiglaze.

Season well, finish with a little butter.

Garnish:

Place four slices of stuffed courgette at the top of each plate, strain the sauce into the middle of the plates and finally set the steak on top.

"Good quality food costs money, if you want it pay! ... If not go without ... it's as simple as that!"

FILLET OF LAMB WITH PORT AND COURGETTE
Serves Two

Ingredients:

1lb	Eye of Meat from Best End of Lamb (boned and trimmed)
1 large	Courgette (grated)
1oz/25g	Butter
2fl.oz/50ml	Stock
Pinch	Garlic
1 tsp	Shallots
2fl.oz/50ml	Brown Sauce
2fl.oz/50ml	Port
Pinch	Rosemary

Garnish:

Fresh Mint and Chopped Tomato

Method:

Seal the seasoned lamb fillet in half the butter. When completely coloured place in the oven for a further 10 minutes. Remove the meat from the pan and place the pan on a high gas. Add the shallots and garlic and cook quickly. Add the port and flame. When this has reduced add the lamb stock and brown sauce, and simmer.

In a separate pan sauté the courgette quickly with the rosemary. Season the sauce and finish with a little butter.

Slice the lamb and arrange in a fan on the plate. Using a pastry ring to form a circle of courgette, at the head of the fan, pass the sauce onto the lamb.

Garnish with fresh mint and chopped tomatoes, and serve.

ROAST FILLET OF BEEF WITH BUTTER SAUCE
Serves Six

Ingredients:

2½-3lb/1.1-1.35kg	Fillet of Beef, centre cut (Château Briand)
	Freshly Ground Black Pepper
3 tbsp	Olive Oil
7oz/200g	Unsalted Butter
4-6 thin cut rashers	Streaky Bacon
1-2 tbsp	White Wine
1	Shallot (finely chopped)
1 sprig	Fresh Tarragon
2	Bay Leaves

Method:

Trim the fillet, bring to room temperature and pat quite dry. Season with pepper only and tie with string in 2-3 places to keep a good shape. Heat the oil in a frying pan and brown the beef all over. Lay it in a roasting tin in which you have melted the butter, and cover with rashers of streaky bacon, adding the wine, shallots, tarragon and bay leaves.

Cook in a very hot oven Gas Mark 9 (240°C, 475°F) for 10 minutes, then baste and lower the temperature to moderate Gas Mark 4 (180°C, 350°F) for a further 15-25 minutes until cooked to your liking.

Check during cooking that the butter is not burning and add another tablespoon of wine if necessary. Remove the beef from the oven and rest somewhere where it will keep warm but not continue cooking, this allows the meat fibres to relax and the juices to spread back through the meat. Pour off the butter juices, remove the sprig of tarragon and the bay leaves and serve with the meat as garnish.

"The assistant manager stood on the big tub of cold thick cooking fat. I passed him the ladder — to no avail, (my first kitchen apprentice chef smile) I could see what would happen ... the lid gave in and slowly he sank up to his knees"
John Benson Smith 1974

SUPREME OF CHICKEN INDONESIENNE
Serves Six

Ingredients:

6 x 5.5-6ozs/ 1drm Supreme Chicken
     1 drm Starch
     5 drm White Wine
    1 drm/8 Curry Powder
     5 drm Pineapple Slices (drained)
    4 drm/8 Chopped Fresh Onion
     1 drm Chopped Fresh Carrot
     1 drm Chopped Fresh Celery
     3 Chopped Fresh Garlic
    1 drm/8 Split Almonds
     2 drm Chopped Chutney
     1 drm Chicken Bouillon
     3 drm Butter
     4 drm Cooking Oil
     Pinch Ground Ginger
     Pinch Ground Corriander
    2.5 pts Water
    12 drm Double Cream
     Salt, Pepper
     Bay Leaves

Pilaff Rice

    14 drm American Long Grain Rice
    1.5 pts Water
     2 drm Butter
    1 drm/8 Chopped Onion
     1 drm Chicken Bouillon
     Seasoning, Bay Leaf

Method:

Chop onion, garlic, celery and carrot very finely.
Place the butter and some of the oil in a saucepan and fry all the vegetables for 3-4 minutes.

Add curry powder and fry slowly for 2-3 minutes.
Add flour and fry for several minutes.
Add water, bouillon, bay leaf, chopped chutney and seasonings; bring to the boil and simmer for 1-1¼ hours.
Coat the chicken supremes with seasoned flour and fry slowly in oil until cooked (2-3 minutes each side). Remove from pan and place in foil.
Place chopped almonds and wine in a pan and bring to the boil.
Cut drained pineapple into julienne.
Place cream in another pan and slowly bring to the boil. Strain the basic sauce through a sieve and add to the cream with the almonds, wine and pineapple.
Thicken with the starch blended with a little water.
Check consistency and seasoning and adjust if necessary.
Pour sauce over the supremes.

Pilaff Rice

Melt the butter and add the chopped onion, fry for several minutes.
Add the rice and fry several minutes.
Add the water, bouillon and seasonings; bring to the boil.
Cover with a tightly fitting lid and place in an oven pre-heated to 400°F and continue cooking for approximately 25 minutes.

By Camillo Zuin
Executive Chef
Trusthouse Forte

LOBSTER SALAD WITH AVOCADO
Serves Six
Main Course

Ingredients:

    3 x 1 lb Lobster
  4oz/100g Lettuce
     2 Avocado Pears
     3 Pink Grapefruits
      Chives

Court Bouillon:

Celery
Carrot
Onion
Bay Leaf
Herbs
White Wine

Sauce:

Virgin Olive Oil
White Vinegar
Salt and Pepper
Juice from Grapefruit

Method:

Prepare the court bouillon and cook the lobster in it for 20 minutes.
Prepare the lettuce, slice the avocado and segment the grapefruits. Separate the grapefruit juice.
Add to the grapefruit juice, salt, pepper, white vinegar and olive oil. Whisk until mixed completely to make a sauce.
Slice the lobster once cooled.

Prepare the serving plate:

Shred the lettuce and place on the base.
Arrange the grapefruit segments and avocado slices alternatively on the lettuce.
Place the sliced lobster on top.
Sprinkle with chopped chives.
Serve with the sauce.

By Camillo Zuin
Executive Chef
Trusthouse Forte

LES SUPREMES DE VOLAILLE TROIS COULEURS
(Breast of Chicken with three colours)
Serves Six

Ingredients:

6ozs/6 x 5.5	Fresh Chicken Supremes
1oz	Onion
1 lb	Aubergines
5ozs	Courgettes
8ozs	Tomatoes
4ozs	Red Peppers
3 drms	Garlic
1 small	Bunch Garlic
1 small	Bunch Tarragon
4ozs	Butter
2ozs	Mozzarella
4 fl.oz	White Wine
4ozs	Oil
1oz	Flour
	Salt
	Pepper

Method:

Take the aubergines, peel, split in half, remove the centre and sprinkle with a little salt. Leave 35-40 minutes in a strainer to drain. The courgettes are then peeled and cut into small dice, also dice the aubergine centres. Place in a strainer, sprinkle with salt and allow to drain for 35-40 minutes. Blanch, skin, de-seed and chop the tomatoes. Peel and finely chop the onion and crush the garlic.

Take a pan, add oil and fry the onion and garlic for 5-6 minutes. Add the diced courgettes, diced aubergine, tomatoes, season and cook for 20 minutes.

Dry the aubergine halves, place in a pan with a little oil and cook in the oven for 15-20 minmutes. When cooked, the filling of courgettes, aubergine and tomatoes is placed in the aubergine halves.

The red peppers are burnt, skinned and cut into the required strips (2" long .5" wide). Put these strips into a pan with oil and seasoning, cook in the oven for 8-10 minutes. The mozzarella cheese is cut to the same size.

A strip of cheese and pepper is then placed on top of the filled aubergine, leaving an equal space between these two for the chopped parsley.

The supremes are trimmed, if necessary, seasoned and lightly floured. They are then fried on each side for 5-6 minutes in a pan containing the oil and butter and flambé the supremes in white wine. Remove the supremes, add butter and the fresh chopped tarragon and parsley. Bring to the boil and check the seasoning.
Place the supremes and aubergines in an 18" silver flat. Just before serving, pour the butter over the whole dish. Serve very hot.

By Camillo Zuin
Executive Chef
Trusthouse Forte

John Benson Smith at the Black Swan

TO CONTINUE

VEGETABLES: IDEAS AND INSPIRATIONS

I seemed to spend an eternity during my levels of training fitting into the role of 'Veg Chef'.

I learnt as an apprentice, mainly from one particular Sous Chef, the delights and surprises of the vegetable and potato. The Rumbler became my right hand man for only a few short months as I quickly learnt how exciting and fascinating this area of the kitchen could be, coupled with the fact that we also made the 'Soup of the Day'.

It was primarily in a time of food fashion, where vegetables, fish and main courses were served with borders of piped potato on vast silver flats ... an era past ... but, I'm sure, to be resurrected again one day.

I am not really a believer in 'al dente' or crisp vegetables, but even though I am not a fashion or whim follower, one must listen to customer dictation and food trends to a certain extent, and healthy eating.

A clean, tender, tasty well braised leek can rival a modern beetroot and peanut mousse any day ... let's be honest, a pan of seasoned, rolling boiling water beats the legs off a modern newfangled steamer!

Wouldn't our children benefit more at school learning about what they eat, and the difference between aubergine, okra and ogen melons and how they could be grown, than hours, days and months of rugby or other equal non-essentials — however I shall not say the same for cricket as my grandfather coached the M.C.C. !!

JOHN BENSON SMITH

TIPS:
— A little sugar in Watercress Soup or Sauce will enhance the flavour.
— Place a clean cloth under chopping board to stop it from moving.
— When using a kitchen hammer/cleaver, work directly over the table legs to lessen the noise.
— Remember the seasons — relate the dishes to the time of year. Ambience and surroundings are important to service of food, give it thought.
— Little things add up to form a jigsaw of success ... success can look like failure half way through ... persevere.
— As a rule, plate your food.
— Clean, hygienic, and always safe.
— We eat the food, not the plate, a simple plain white canvas to paint on is most efficient.
— Taste, balance and presentation should all mix.
— Pancakes and Yorkshire Pudding are the same mix.

METHODS OF VEGETABLE COOKERY

Boiling

Boiling is the cooking of foods in a liquid, usually stock or water. The temperature at which food is cooked is controlled by the temperature of the boiling liquid and this temperature will not increase once the boiling point is reached. Therefore, simmering (or gentle boiling) should be allowed to take place, to reduce damage that may take place during rapid boiling.

In order to retain flavour, colour and nutrients, vegetables should be cooked as freshly and quickly as possible.

In general, vegetables grown above the ground (green vegetables) should be cooked in boiling salted water or stock. Vegetables grown below the ground (root vegetables) are started in cold salted water or stock with the exception of new potatoes.

Stewing

Stewing is the slow cooking of foods in the smallest quantity of water, stock or sauce in which the ingredients are normally cut up. The food and the liquid are served together, in this way none of the juices are lost.

Stewed vegetables, for example, Ratatouille and French Style Peas can be cooked either in a covered stewpan or casserole on the stove top or in a moderate oven. This method differs from boiling in that much less liquid is used and the cooking temperature is approximately 10°F less.

Braising

Braising is a combination of roasting and stewing in a pan with a tight fitting lid (casserole or cocotte — the lid is essential in preventing evaporation and enabling the food not only to retain its own flavour, but also the flavours of the commodities used in the cooking).

All vegetables that are braised, are blanched in boiling water before braising commences. Examples are — onions, leeks, lettuce, endive, celery, fennel, cabbage and okra.

Roasting

Roasting is the cooking by radiant heat with the aid of fat in the form of basting every 20-30 minutes.

Roasting can be carried out in two ways: however, only one way is suitable for vegetables. This is by the convection oven method and the only vegetable that is cooked in this way, is parsnips.

Baking

Baking is the cooking of foods by dry radiant heat in an oven.

The action of dry heat is modified by steam which is the result of the food water content being cooked.

Examples of vegetables cooked in this way are: stuffed tomatoes, onions, stuffed pimentoes and courgettes.

Grilling

Grilling is a very fast method of cooking as the high temperature radiant heat, or direct heat used can be maintained throughout the cooking process. Due to the intense heat, grilling is only suitable for certain vegetables that have been brushed with oil or butter.
Examples are: tomatoes and mushrooms.

Shallow Frying
This is cooking in shallow fat/oil and in a frying pan, sauté pan, or on a griddle plate. As a general rule, the presentation side of the food being cooked should always be fried first, as this side will have the better appearance.

Examples are: aubergine, courgettes, vegetable croquettes, mushrooms and tomatoes.

Deep Frying

This is cooking in a Friture in deep oil.

It is important that the selected oil can be raised to a high temperature without burning.

As a general rule, vegetables cooked by this method are coated with one of the following: flour, batter or breadcrumbs.

Examples are: cauliflower fritters, aubergines, onion rings and vegetable croquettes.

Sauté / Stir Fry

These terms are used when vegetables are tossed in a frying pan or wok with a minmimum of fat or oil, allowing the vegetables to be cooked as quickly and crisply as possible.

Examples are: mushrooms, mange tout, courgettes, leeks, onions, peppers, mooli and beansprouts.

Pressure Steaming

This is a method of cooking in moist heat, but faster than boiling methods. The process is carried out in a steamer with a minumum pressure of $1\frac{1}{4}$ kg/cm^2.

Modern high speed steamers can be used for 'batch' cooking, which means the frequent cooking of smaller quantities of vegetables throughout the service period.

Steaming is a method that can be applied to all green and root vegetables.

"Even the most prolific chefs would have problems altering John's recipes for the better"
Pressmans Diary

Artichoke Jerusalem
Crisp, sweet and ivory white flesh. The artichoke should be a regular shape, measuring up to 3 inches (7.5cm) long and 1 inch (2.5cm) across.

Aubergine
Bright, shining purple skins that are unblemished. Test by gently pressing the skin, they should have a 'live' resilient feel.

Beans (Broad)
Uniform, bright green pods, free from black markings and blemishes. Avoid beans over 6 inches (15cm) long as the beans will lose their soft and tender texture. Avoid shrivelled dry looking beans.

Beans (French)
Young beans should be slender, stringless and of a bright green colour. The bean should be crisp, have unblemished skin and be 5 inches (12.5cm) maximum in length.

Beans (Runner)
Flat, straight, bright green pods. When the bean matures the skin becomes tough and the outer casing rather stringy. Test for freshness by snapping into two, listen for a crisp snap. The insides should be fresh and juicy.

Broccoli/Calabrese
Green and purple types are available. Look for non-woody stems and fresh crisp leaves. The heads should not exceed 3 inches (7.5cm) in diameter.

Brussels Sprouts
Dark, green, compact and firm to touch. Avoid yellow and wilting leaves.
Brussels — 1 inch (2.5cm) in diameter
Button — ½ to ¾ inch (1.25 to 1.875cm) in diameter.
The nutty flavour of the sprout is greatly improved by frost.

Cabbage (Red)
Dark red in colour with shiny leaves. The cabbage should be in good bloom and not split or cut. It should be heavy for the size, firm and crisp.

Carrots (New)
New season carrots should have their green fresh tops intact and be bright orange in colour. The flesh should be crisp and well shaped, clean and unblemished. Avoid them if they have green crowns.

Carrots (Old/Summer)
Well shaped with a good orange colour. The skin should be smooth and unblemished. Avoid carrots with woody cores and mis-shaped tips, and green crowns.

Cauliflower
Fresh green leaves, surrounding a firm white head, with no blemishes or bruises. The base of the stalk should be clean and white with tiny flowers forming the head which should not be feathery. If the head has been exposed to sunlight, rain or frost it will turn to a yellowish shade, this only affects the appearance not the taste.

Celeriac
Firm and heavy for the size (if it is light in weight, the flesh will be airy and spongy). Light brown in colour, rough and ridged skin that should be free from blemishes and bruises. Do not waste the leaves, they are excellent to flavour stocks and soups.

Celery
Thick and plump base with clean green and golden stalks. (The main crop of celery is covered with earth to keep the stalks white, ensure it is well washed in salted water). The green leafy tops should be fresh and not wilting.

Chicory
Chicory is grown in the dark to produce its crisp white leaves. Ensure that the leaves are tight together, unmarked and crisp. A green line at the top of the chicory usually means that the plant will be bitter.

Courgette/Zucchini
The courgette/zucchini should be 3 to 4 inches (7.5 to 10cm) long, smooth, tender and unblemished skins. It should be tender enough for the skin to be pierced by the fingernail and should be of uniform shape.

Fennel
Pale green or white coloured bulb. Avoid any that are dark green or yellowing.

Leeks
Choose smaller leeks as they will be more tender. They should look well balanced at the root with a crisp green top.

Mange Tout
Bright green in colour, crisp to the touch. Avoid pods with over-formed peas and rust spots.

Marrow
Best when under 1 kilo at 12 inches long, with firm smooth skin and dull bloom to skin.

Mooli
Conical in shape with no roots. It should be firm, smooth and have unblemished skin. Best at 12 inches (30cm) long and 3 inches (7.5cm) in diameter.

Mushrooms
White to cream in colour. The mushroom should have unopened caps with delicate beige to pink gills, free from mould and blemishes. The best size is 1 inch (2.5cm) or under in diameter.

Okra
Dark green in colour with a crisp pod. Avoid any that are discoloured or stringy. Best cooked slightly under-ripe.

Onions
Firm to touch with bright, dry, unblemished skins. Avoid any that may show signs of sprouting.

Parsnips
Regular uniform shape without side roots. It should be clean and crisp in appearance. Avoid parsnips with soft brown patches at the crown.

Peppers
Firm, crisp and glossy, neither dull nor wrinkled, unblemished or split. Best at 3½ inches (8.75cm) long and 3 inches (7.5cm) in diameter.

Salsify
6 to 8 inches (15 to 20cm) in length, 1 inch (2.5cm) at the widest part. The flesh should be white, crisp and unblemished; the skin intact. Handle carefully as they are very delicate and bruise easily.

Spinach
Bright glossy green leaves, crisp but moist. The stalks should be crisp and well trimmed.

Sweetcorn
In leaf: Look for bright leaves that are tightly wrapped around the cob with brown wilting tassel (silks).

Out of leaf: Plump, full bright golden yellow colour which excludes milk juice when pierced with thumbnail. Best at 6-9 inches (10-17.5cm) long.

Tomato
Firm, bright red, glossy skin. Uniform in size and shape. Avoid yellow skinned tomatoes.

ARTICHOKE Jerusalem

ARTICHOKES WITH ORANGE

Preparation:

Scrub the artichoke under running cold water to remove any surplus dirt.
Peel away any discoloured and knobbly parts.
Place the artichoke under cold water with lemon juice.

Method:

Peel thinly and cut into even-sized pieces.
Cook the artichokes in boiling salted water until tender.
Drain well.
Dress into hot buttered vegetable dish.
Coat with orange sauce (see recipe).

ARTICHOKES WITH MADAGASCAN PEPPER

Preparation:

Scrub the artichoke under running cold water to remove any surplus dirt.
Peel away any discoloured knobbly parts.
Place the artichoke into cold water with lemon juice.

Method

Peel thinly and cut into even-sized pieces.
Cook the artichokes in boiling salted water until tender.
Drain well.
Dress into hot buttered vegetable dish.
Coat with green peppercorn sauce (see recipe).

ARTICHOKES WITH MUSTARD

Preparation:

Scrub the artichoke under running cold water to remove any surplus dirt.
Peel away any discoloured and knobbly parts.
Place the artichoke under cold water with lemon juice.

Method:

Peel thinly and cut into even-sized pieces.
Cook the artichokes in boiling salted water until tender.
Drain well.
Dress into hot buttered vegetable dish.
Coat with mustard seed sauce (see recipe).

AUBERGINE

AUBERGINE FRITTERS

Preparation:

Remove the crown and leaves around it.
Cut the aubergine into ¼" slices.
Place the aubergine in a colander and sprinkle the cut surface with salt and leave for 30 minutes.
This will drain out the excess juice (you will see beads of moisture forming).
Rinse the slices thoroughly and pat dry with kitchen paper.

Method:

Dip seasoned aubergine into flour and batter (see recipe).
Cook the aubergine in hot oil 275° until crisp and golden.
Drain well on kitchen paper.
Dress into hot service dishes.

AUBERGINE IN TOMATO AND GARLIC SAUCE

Preparation:

Remove the crown and leaves around it.
Cut the aubergine into ¼" slices.
Place the aubergine in a colander and sprinkle the cut surface with salt and leave for 30 minutes.
This will drain out the excess juice (you will see beads of moisture forming).
Rinse the slices thoroughly and pat dry with kitchen paper.

Method:

Simmer the aubergine in a little oil with onion and chopped garlic until half cooked.
Season with seasoning mixture (see recipe).
Add chopped peeled tomatoes.
Return to simmer until cooked.
Dress into hot buttered service dishes.

STUFFED AUBERGINE

Preparation:

Remove the crown and leaves around it.
Cut in half lengthwise.
Score the flesh criss-cross with a sharp knife.

Method:

Place seasoned aubergine face down on a lightly oiled tray.
Bake in the oven until tender.
Once cooked scoop out the flesh.
Mix well with the same amount of stuffing mixture (see recipe).
Place the mixture back into the skin.
Return to oven to reheat.
Place into hot vegetable dishes.
Serve with a cordon of madeira sauce (see recipe).

BEANS~Broad

BROAD BEANS IN CREAM SAUCE

Preparation:

Shell beans and wash in salted water.
Remove the inner shells if tough.

Method:

Cook beans in boiling salted water.
Drain well.
Bind with cream sauce (see recipe).
Correct the seasoning with seasoning
mixture (see recipe).
Dress into hot buttered vegetable dish.

BROAD BEANS IN PARSLEY SAUCE

Preparation:

Shell beans and wash in salted water.
Remove the inner shells if tough.

Method:

Cook beans in boiling salted water.
Drain well.
Bind with parsley sauce (see recipe).
Correct the seasoning with seasoning
mixture (see recipe).
Dress into hot buttered vegetable dish.

BROAD BEANS WITH DILL

Preparation:

Shell beans and wash in salted water.
Remove inner shells if tough.

Method:

Cook beans in boiling salted water.
Drain well.
Toss beans in foaming butter.
Add liberal amounts of chopped dill.
Correct the seasoning.
Dress into hot buttered vegetable dish.

BEANS~French

FRENCH BEANS WITH HAZELNUTS

Preparation:

Top and tail the beans — this is best done
by hand, rather than with a knife, less
wastage is incurred.
Wash beans in cold salted water.

Method:

Cook beans in boiling salted water.
Drain well.
Melt a knob of butter in a sauteuse until
foaming.
Add the French beans and chopped
hazelnuts and gently toss together.
Correct the seasoning.
Place into a hot buttered vegetable dish.

FRENCH BEANS IN BACON

Preparation:

Top and tail the beans — this is best done
by hand, rather than with a knife, less
wastage is incurred.
Wash beans in cold salted water.

Method:

Cook beans in boiling salted water.
Refresh under cold running water.
Drain well.
Wrap a rasher of bacon around small
bunches.
Trim off ends to keep tidy.
Place onto to an oven tray.
Brush with butter.
Place in the oven until bacon is cooked.
Serve in a hot buttered vegetable dish.

FRENCH BEANS WITH THYME

Preparation:

Top and tail the beans — this is best done
by hand, rather than with a knife, less
wastage is incurred.
Wash beans in cold salted water.

Method:

Cook beans in boiling salted water.
Drain well.
Melt a knob of butter in a sauteuse until
foaming.
Add the French beans and chopped thyme
and gently toss together.
Correct the seasoning.
Place into hot buttered vegetable dish.

RUNNER BEANS WITH HERBS

Preparation:

Top and tail and remove the stringy sides with a sharp knife.
Cut diagonally into 1″ lengths.
Wash in cold salted water.

Method:

Cook beans in boiling salted water.
Drain well.
Melt butter in a thick-bottomed pan.
Add the runner beans and chopped herbs.
Toss together.
Correct seasoning with seasoning mixture (see recipe).
Dress into hot buttered vegetable dish.

RUNNER BEANS WITH BACON

Preparation:

Top and tail and remove the stringy sides with a sharp knife.
Cut diagonally into 1″ lengths.
Wash in cold salted water.

Method:

Cook beans in boiling salted water.
Melt butter in a thick-bottomed pan.
Add lardons of bacon and quickly cook.
Add runner beans and toss together.
Correct seasoning with seasoning mixture (see recipe).
Serve in hot buttered vegetable dish.

RUNNER BEANS WITH SOFT GREEN PEPPERCORNS

Preparation:

Top and tail and remove the stringy sides with a sharp knife.
Cut diagonally into 1″ lengths.
Wash in cold salted water.

Method:

Cook beans in boiling salted water.
Drain well.
Bind with green peppercorn sauce (see recipe).
Correct seasoning with seasoning mixture (see recipe).
Dress into hot buttered vegetable dish.

SUBRIC OF BROCCOLI WITH CHEESE SAUCE

Preparation:

Heading varieties are trimmed and broken into florets and cooked whole.
For sprouting varieties, trim the base of the stalk, if they are very large, cut into two, lengthways.
Wash in cold salted water.

Method:

Cook the broccoli in boiling salted water.
Drain well.
Purée the broccoli in a food processor.
Season with the seasoning mixture (see recipe).
Add 4 eggs per pint of broccoli purée and 2-3 tablespoons of cream.
Mix well and pour into buttered dariol moulds.
Poach in a bain marie 15-20 minutes.
Turn out into a hot vegetable dish.
Finish with a cordon of cheese sauce (see recipe).

BROCCOLI WITH LEMON SAUCE

Preparation:

Heading varieties are trimmed and broken into florets and cooked whole.
For sprouting varieties, trim the base of the stalk, if they are very large, cut into two, lengthways.
Wash in cold salted water.

Method:

Cook the broccoli in boiling salted water.
Drain well.
Place into hot buttered vegetable dish.
Coat with lemon sauce (see recipe).

BROCCOLI WITH HAZELNUTS

Preparation:

Heading varieties are trimmed and broken into florets and cooked whole.
For sprouting varieties, trim the base of the stalk, if they are very large, cut into two, lengthways.
Wash in cold salted water.

Method:

Cook the broccoli in boiling salted water.
Drain well.
Dress into hot buttered vegetable dish.
Pour over chopped hazelnuts that have been tossed in nut brown butter.

BRUSSELS SPROUTS

SUBRIC OF BRUSSELS SPROUTS WITH CREAM SAUCE

Preparation:

Remove the outer leaves and remove the stem.
Cut a cross in the stem to ensure even cooking.
Wash thoroughly in cold salted water, drain well.

Method:

Cook sprouts in boiling salted water.
Drain well.
Purée in a food processor.
Season with seasoning mixture (see recipe).
Add four eggs per pint of purée and 2-3 tablespoons of cream.
Mix well, pour into buttered dariol moulds.
Poach in a bain marie 15-20 minutes.
Turn out into a hot vegetable dish.
Finish with a cordon of cream sauce (see recipe).

BRUSSELS SPROUTS WITH CHESTNUTS

Preparation:

Remove the outer leaves and remove the stem.
Cut a cross in the stem to ensure even cooking.
Wash thoroughly in cold salted water, drain well.

Method:

Cook sprouts in boiling salted water.
Drain well.
Toss in butter with chopped cooked chestnuts.
Dress into hot buttered vegetable dishes.

BRUSSELS SPROUTS WITH BACON

Preparation:

Remove the outer leaves and remove the stem.
Cut a cross in the stem to ensure even cooking.
Wash thoroughly in cold salted water, drain well.

Method:

Cook sprouts in boiling salted water.
Drain well.
Melt butter in sauteuse, add brussels and strips of cooked bacon.
Season well with seasoning mixture (see recipe).
Dress into hot buttered vegetable dishes.

CABBAGE~Red

BRAISED WEDGES IN ORANGE JUICE

Preparation:

Remove the outer leaves and cut cabbage in half.
Cut each half into 4-6 wedges.
Wash thoroughly in cold salted water, drain well.

Method:

Blanch wedges in boiling salted water for 3-4 minutes.
Lay wedges into suitable dish for braising.
Pour a mixture of orange juice and chicken stock to half cover the cabbage.
Season with seasoning mixture (see recipe).
Cover with tight fitting lid. Braise until tender.
Serve in hot vegetable dish.

BRAISED STUFFED RED CABBAGE

Preparation:

Remove the outer leaves.
Wash thoroughly in cold salted water, drain well.

Method:

Blanch cabbage leaves in boiling salted water for 4-5 minutes and refresh in cold water.
Fill leaves with stuffing mixture (see recipe).
Form into dome shape with the help of a ladle.
Place into suitable dish for braising.
Pour a mixture of orange juice and chicken stock into the dish to half cover the cabbage.
Cover with a tight fitting lid and braise until tender.
Dress in hot vegetable dish.

RED CABBAGE BRAISED WITH APPLES AND RAISINS

Preparation:

Remove the outer leaves and cut cabbage in half.
Cut each half into 2 pieces, remove core and centre stalks.
Wash thoroughly in cold salted water, drain well.

Method:

Shred cabbage finely.
Melt butter in large pan, add the cabbage and sweat lightly.
Add a ¼pt vinegar, 2 apples diced and 2oz raisins per cabbage.
Season with seasoning mixture (see recipe).
Cover with a tight fitting lid. Braise until tender.
Serve in hot vegetable dish.

CABBAGE ~ White

STUFFED CABBAGE WITH MADEIRA SAUCE

Preparation:

Remove the outer leaves from the cabbage.
Remove thick centre stalk.
Wash thoroughly in cold salted water, drain well.

Method:

Blanch the leaves in boiling salted water for 3-4 minutes.
Refresh under cold water and drain well.
Fill leaves with stuffing mixture (see recipe).
Form into equal sized domes with the help of a ladle.
Place into a suitable dish for braising.
Pour chicken stock to half cover the cabbage.
Cover with tight fitting lid and braise until tender.
Serve in hot buttered vegetable dish with a cordon of madeira sauce (see recipe).

CABBAGE WITH HAM AND CREAM

Preparation:

Remove the outer leaves and cut cabbage in half.
Cut each half into 2 pieces, remove core and centre stalks.
Wash thoroughly in cold salted water, drain well.

Method:

Shred cabbage finely.
Cook in boiling salted water.
Drain well.
Add chopped ham and cream sauce (see recipe) to cabbage.
Mix well.
Season with seasoning mixture (see recipe).
Dress into hot buttered vegetable dish.

WHITE CABBAGE STIR-FRIED WITH PEPPERS

Preparation:

Remove the outer leaves and cut cabbage in half.
Cut each half into 2 pieces, remove core and centre stalks.
Wash thoroughly in cold salted water, drain well.

Method:

Finely shred cabbage.
Blanch in boiling salted water.
Drain well.
Toss in butter with strips of red, green and yellow peppers.
Season with seasoning mixture (see recipe).
Serve in hot buttered vegetable dish.

CARROTS

CARROTS IN DILL SAUCE

Preparation:

New —
Remove the crown and tip from root and scrub thoroughly.
Maincrop —
Remove the crown and tip from root and wash in cold water.
Peel thinly.

Method:

Cut carrots into batons, or slices.
Cook in boiling salted water with a little sugar.
Drain well.
Dress into hot service dishes.
Coat with dill sauce (see recipe).

HONEY GLAZED CARROTS

Preparation:

New —
Remove the crown and tip from root and scrub thoroughly.
Maincrop —
Remove the crown and tip from root and wash in cold water.
Peel thinly.

Method:

Cut carrots into batons, or slices.
Cook in boiling salted water with a little sugar.
Drain well.
Melt a drop of butter in a sauteuse until foaming.
Add the carrots and quickly toss.
Add honey, 1oz/2lb carrots.
Correct the seasoning.
Dress into hot service dish.

CARROT PURÉE

Preparation:

New —
Remove the crown and tip from root and scrub thoroughly.
Maincrop —
Remove the crown and tip from root and wash in cold water.
Peel thinly.

Method:

Cut carrots into even-sized pieces.
Barely cover with water, add seasoning mixture (see recipe).
Simmer until tender.
Drain well.
Purée in a food processor.
Return to the heat, mix in a knob of butter.
Correct the seasoning.
Dress into hot service dishes.

CAULIFLOWER

CAULIFLOWER POLONAISE

Preparation:

Cut away the outside green leaves, leaving only the smaller ones.
Break into florets.
Steep thoroughly in cold salted water to remove any grit and insects.

Method:

Cook the florets of cauliflower in boiling salted water.
Drain well.
Dress into a hot service dish.
Coat with polonaise mixture (see recipe).

CAULIFLOWER WITH DILL SAUCE

Preparation:

Cut away the outside green leaves, leaving only the smaller ones.
Break into florets.
Steep thoroughly in cold salted water to remove any grit and insects.

Method:

Cook the florets of cauliflower in boiling salted water.
Drain well.
Dress into a hot service dish.
Coat with dill sauce (see recipe).

CAULIFLOWER FRITTERS

Preparation:

Cut away the outside green leaves, leaving only the smaller ones.
Break into florets.
Steep thoroughly in cold salted water to remove any grit and insects.

Method:

Cook the florets of cauliflower in boiling salted water and retain crispness.
Drain well.
Roll in seasoned flour.
Dip in batter mix (see recipe).
Deep fry in hot oil 250° - 275°C until crisp and golden.
Drain on kitchen paper.
Dress into hot service dish.
Dust with paprika.

CELERIAC

CELERIAC IN PARSLEY SAUCE

Preparation:

Scrub thoroughly and cut off all the roots.
Peel to remove skin and knobbly parts.
Place immediately in cold water with a little lemon juice to prevent discolouration.

Method:

Cut celeriac into batons.
Cook in boiling salted water.
Drain well.
Fold gently into parsley sauce (see recipe).
Place into hot buttered service dish.

CELERIAC WITH APPLE AND CIDER SAUCE

Preparation:

Scrub thoroughly and cut off all the roots.
Peel to remove skin and knobbly parts.
Place immediately in cold water with a little lemon juice to prevent discolouration.

Method:

Cut celeriac into batons.
Cook in boiling salted water.
Drain well.
Braise in madeira sauce with cider (see recipe).
Finish with batons of apple at the last moment.
Dress into hot buttered vegetable dish.

CELERIAC WITH SOFT GREEN PEPPERCORNS

Preparation:

Scrub thoroughly and cut off all the roots.
Peel to remove skin and knobbly parts.
Place immediately in cold water with a little lemon juice to prevent discolouration.

Method:

Cut celeriac into ½″ dice.
Cook in boiling salted water.
Drain well.
Gently fold into green peppercorn sauce (see recipe).
Dress into hot buttered vegetable dish.

CELERY

BRAISED CELERY HEARTS

Preparation:

Trim off the root and the top of the leaves (retain as these can be used in soups). Separate the stalks and leave to soak in cold salted water for 10-15 minutes. Scrub thoroughly and rinse well.

Method:

Cut 4″ of heart from the celery, reserve rest for other dishes.
Blanch in boiling water for 4-5 minutes.
Drain well.
Place into suitable dish for braising.
Half cover with chicken stock.
Cover with a tight fitting lid and braise until tender.
Dress into service dish.
Coat with madeira sauce (see recipe).

STUFFED CELERY

Preparation:

Trim off the root and the top of the leaves (retain as these can be used in soups). Separate the stalks and leave to soak in cold salted water for 10-15 minutes. Scrub thoroughly and rinse well.

Method:

Cut celery into 3″ lengths.
¾ cook in boiling salted water.
Drain well and reserve the cooking liquor.
Sandwich two pieces together with stuffing mixture (see recipe).
Place into suitable dish for braising.
Pour cooking liquid ⅓ the way up the celery.
Cover with a tight fitting lid. Braise until tender.
Dress into service dish, coat with cream sauce (see recipe).
Sprinkle with cheese and white breadcrumbs and glaze.

CELERY GLAZED

Preparation:

Trim off the root and the top of the leaves (retain as these can be used in soups). Separate the stalks and leave to soak in cold salted water for 10-15 minutes. Scrub thoroughly and rinse well.

Method:

Cook celery in boiling salted water.
Cut into 3″ lengths. Place into service dish.
Coat with cheese sauce (see recipe).
Sprinkle with a mixture of white breadcrumbs and cheese.
Glaze under a hot salamander.

CHICORY

CHICORY ITALIAN STYLE

Preparation:

Trim the stem and carefully scoop out part of the core with a sharp pointed knife. Wash in cold salted water, do not leave in the water as this tends to increase the bitterness.

Method:

Place in a well buttered casserole or pan that is suitable to place in the oven. Season lightly with the seasoning mixture (see recipe).
Add the juice of a half lemon per lb. Add 1oz of butter per lb and a few drops of stock.
Cover with a buttered paper and the lid.
Cook gently in a moderate oven 150°-200°C for approximately 1 hour.
Dress neatly into service dishes.
Coat with Sauce Italian (see recipe).

BRAISED CHICORY IN MADEIRA SAUCE

Preparation:

Trim the stem and carefully scoop out part of the core with a sharp pointed knife. Wash in cold salted water, do not leave in the water as this tends to increase the bitterness.

Method:

Place in a well buttered casserole or pan that is suitable to place in the oven. Season lightly with seasoning mixture (see recipe).
Add the juice of half a lemon per lb. Add 1oz of butter per lb and a few drops of stock.
Cover with a buttered paper and the lid.
Cook gently in a moderate oven 150°-200°C for approximately 1 hour.
Dress neatly into service dishes.
Surround with a cordon of madeira sauce (see recipe).

CHICORY WITH LEMON SAUCE

Preparation:

Trim the stem and carefully scoop out part of the core with a sharp pointed knife. Wash in cold salted water, do not leave in the water as this tends to increase the bitterness.

Method:

Place in a well buttered casserole or pan that is suitable to place in the oven. Season lightly with the seasoning mixture (see recipe).
Add the juice of half a lemon per lb. Add 1oz of butter per lb and a few drops of stock.
Cover with a buttered paper and the lid.
Cook gently in a moderate oven 150°-200°C for approximately 1 hour.
Dress neatly into service dishes.
Coat with lemon sauce (see recipe).

BABY CORN

STIR-FRIED BABY CORN

Preparation:

Trim off stalks.
Wash in salted water.

Method:

Blanch corn in boiling salted water 3-4 minutes.
Drain well.
Slice corn at a slight angle to give even sized pieces.
Toss in hot vegetable oil with julienne of peppers and onions.
Season with seasoning mixture (see recipe).
Dress into hot buttered service dish.

HONEY GLAZED BABY CORN

Preparation:

Trim off stalks.
Wash in salted water.

Method:

Blanch corn in boiling salted water 4-5 minutes.
Toss in nut brown butter.
Pour over a little honey.
Allow corn to brown slightly.
Dress into hot service dishes.

BABY CORN WITH LEMON

Preparation:

Trim off stalks.
Wash in salted water.

Method:

Cook in boiling salted water.
Drain well.
Roll in hot molten butter.
Add lemon juice and blanched lemon zest.
Correct seasoning with seasoning mixture (see recipe).
Dress into hot buttered vegetable dish.

COURGETTE

COURGETTE GLAZED

Preparation:

Top and tail each courgette.
Wash in cold salted water, drain well.
Cut according to the recipe.

Method:

Quickly cook the courgette in boiling salted water.
Drain in a colander to remove all excess liquid.
Dress into a hot buttered service dish.
Mask with cheese sauce (see recipe).
Sprinkle with a mixture of grated cheese and white breadcrumbs.
Brown under salamander.

BAKED COURGETTES

Preparation:

Top and tail each courgette.
Wash in cold salted water, drain well.
Cut according to the recipe.

Method:

Cut courgettes in half lengthways.
Quickly blanche the courgettes in boiling salted water for a few seconds.
Drain in a colander to remove all excess liquid.
Lay them cut side uppermost on a buttered seasoned baking tray.
Top them with the herb and garlic mixture (see recipe).
Place in a hot oven 200°-250°C for 15-20 minutes.
Dress into a hot service dish and sprinkle with parsley.

COURGETTES WITH ROSEMARY

Preparation:

Top and tail each courgette.
Wash in cold salted water, drain well.
Cut according to the recipe.

Method:

Thinly slice the courgettes.
Melt butter in a thick bottomed frying pan until foaming.
Add the courgettes, season with seasoning mixture (see recipe).
Toss them in butter with fresh rosemary until crisp and lightly golden.
Dress into a hot serving dish.

FENNEL

FENNEL WITH CAPER SAUCE

Preparation:

Trim the root end from the bulb and the stalk end (reserve any feathery leaves to use as garnish or for soups, etc).
Place prepared fennel in a bowl of water with lemon juice to prevent discoloration.

Method:

Cook in boiling salted water 15-20 minutes until cooked.
Drain well and cut into portions 2-3 per bulb.
Place into hot service dishes.
Coat with caper sauce (see recipe).
Sprinkle with chopped parsley.

FENNEL IN ORANGE

Preparation:

Trim the root end from the bulb and the stalk end (reserve any feathery leaves to use as garnish or for soups, etc).
Place prepared fennel in a bowl of water with lemon juice to prevent discoloration.

Method:

Blanch the fennel for 2-3 minutes in boiling salted water.
Drain well and cut into portions, season with seasoning mixture (see recipe).
Place in a dish suitable for braising, 2/3 cover with a good stock.
Cover with buttered foil and braise in a moderate oven 150°-200°C for 1 hour.
Place into hot service dish and coat with orange sauce (see recipe).

FENNEL BRAISED IN MADEIRA SAUCE

Preparation:

Trim the root end from the bulb and the stalk end (reserve any feathery leaves to use as garnish or for soups, etc).
Place prepared fennel in a bowl of water with lemon juice to prevent discoloration.

Method:

Blanch the fennel for 2-3 minutes in salted boiling water.
Drain well and cut into portions, season with the seasoning mixture (see recipe).
Place in a dish suitable for braising, 2/3 cover with a good stock.
Cover with buttered foil and braise in a moderate oven 150°-200°C for 1 hour.
Place into hot service dish and surround with a cordon of madeira sauce (see recipe).

LEEKS

LEEKS IN CREAM SAUCE

Preparation:

Trim the root and top leaving 2-3″ of green.
Cut a slit through the centre lengthways.
Wash thoroughly under cold running water to remove all grit and soil, drain well.

Method:

Tie the leeks into bundles.
Place in boiling salted water for 10 minutes approximately.
Remove from pan and allow to drain.
Fold leeks neatly.
Dress into hot service dishes.
Coat with cream sauce (see recipe).

LEEKS SAUTÉD WITH GINGER

Preparation:

Trim the root and top leaving 2-3″ of green.
Cut a slit through the centre lengthways.
Wash thoroughly under cold running water to remove all grit and soil, drain well.

Method:

Blanch in boiling salted water for 2-3 minutes.
Drain well in a colander.
Melt butter in a thick-bottomed pan until foaming.
Add the leeks and a little shredded root ginger.
Season with the seasoning mixture (see recipe).
Toss quickly in the butter until just cooked.
Dress into hot service dishes.

LEEKS GLAZED

Preparation:

Trim the root and top leaving 2-3″ of green.
Cut a slit through the centre lengthways.
Wash thoroughly under cold running water to remove all grit and soil, drain well.

Method:

Tie the leeks into bundles.
Place in boiling salted water for 10 minutes approximately.
Remove from pan and allow to drain.
Fold leeks neatly.
Dress into hot service dishes.
Coat with cheese sauce (see recipe).
Sprinkle with a mixture of grated cheese and white breadcrumbs.
Quickly brown under the grill.

MANGE TOUT

MARROW

MANGE TOUT WITH LEMON AND CREAM

Preparation:

Wash in cold salted water, drain well.
Top and tail the pods, removing any side
strings.

Method:

Quickly blanch the mange tout in boiling
salted water.
Melt butter in a thick-bottomed pan until
foaming.
Add the mange toute, seasoning mixture
(see recipe), grated lemon zest and quickly
toss to reheat.
Pour in a little double cream.
Serve in a hot service dish.

MANGE TOUT POLONAISE

Preparation:

Wash in cold salted water, drain well.
Top and tail the pods, removing any side
strings.

Method:

Quickly blanch the mange tout in boiling
salted water.
Melt butter in a thick-bottomed pan until
foaming.
Add the mange toute, seasoning mixture
(see recipe), and quickly toss in butter.
Place in hot service dish.
Sprinkle with polonaise mixture (see
recipe).

STIR-FRIED MANGE TOUT

Preparation:

Wash in cold salted water, drain well.
Top and tail the pods, removing any side
strings.

Method:

Quickly toss the mange tout in a little
walnut oil.
Add a julienne of red and green peppers,
root ginger and spring onions.
Quickly cook over a high temperature.
season with a little seasoning mixture (see
recipe).
Dress in a hot service dish.

MARROW IN DILL SAUCE

Preparation:

Wash the outside skin.
Cut in half crosswise, if the marrow is to be
stuffed, peel, scoop out the seeds and
centre fibre.
Cut according to recipe.

Method:

Dice the marrow and boil lightly in salted
water.
Drain well in a colander.
Place into a hot service dish.
Coat with dill sauce (see recipe).

STUFFED MARROW SLICES

Preparation:

Wash the outside skin.
Cut in half crosswise, if the marrow is to be
stuffed, peel, scoop out the seeds and
centre fibre.
Cut according to recipe.

Method:

Place the marrow rings on a buttered dish.
Fill the rings with stuffing (see recipe).
Add a few drops of stock.
Cover with a lid.
Place into a medium oven 150°-200°C for
45-60 minutes.
Serve in hot vegetable dish with a cordon
of tomato and basil sauce (see recipe).

MARROW FRITTERS

Preparation:

Wash the outside skin.
Cut in half crosswise, if the marrow is to be
stuffed, peel, scoop out the seeds and
centre fibre.
Cut according to recipe.

Method:

Cut marrow into strips.
Blanch in boiling salted water 3-4 minutes.
Drain well and place on kitchen paper to
dry.
Roll the marrow in seasoned flour.
Dip into batter mixture (see recipe).
Deep fry in hot oil at 350°-376°C until
crisp and golden.
Dress into hot serving dish.

MOOLI

MOOLI BAKERS STYLE

Preparation:

Wash, remove crown and root tip.
Peel thinly.
Cut as per recipe.

Method:

Cut the mooli into 2mm slices.
Finely slice the onions — 8oz/lb of mooli.
Season stock with seasoning mixture (see recipe).
Neatly arrange, overlapping slices into a suitable dish for braising.
Barely cover with stock.
Brush with butter.
Place into a moderate oven 150°-200°C for 1 hour.
Dress into a hot vegetable dish.

MOOLI STIR-FRIED WITH CASHEWS

Preparation:

Wash, remove crown and root tip.
Peel thinly.
Cut as per recipe.

Method:

Cut the mooli into batons 1½″ × ¼″ × ¼″.
Heat vegetable oil in a thick-bottomed pan until a haze appears.
Add the mooli batons and quickly stir-fry.
Season with seasoning mixture (see recipe).
Add a few cashew nuts and chopped fresh coriander.
Dress into hot service dishes.

MOOLI IN TOMATO AND BASIL SAUCE

Preparation:

Wash, remove crown and root tip.
Peel thinly.
Cut as per recipe.

Method:

Cut the mooli into batons 1½″ × ½″ × ½″.
Place into boiling salted water until just cooked.
Drain well.
Dress into a hot service dish.
Coat with tomato and basil sauce (see recipe).

MUSHROOMS

MUSHROOMS WITH BACON AND CORIANDER

Preparation:

Wash mushrooms in salted water quickly, drain well.
Trim stalks at base.

Method:

Place butter into thick-bottomed pan and melt until foaming.
Add lardons of bacon and quickly fry.
Add the button mushrooms and season with the seasoning mixture (see recipe).
Toss mushrooms in the butter until firm and golden.
Sprinkle with ground coriander.
Dress into hot service dish.

MUSHROOMS IN OATMEAL

Preparation:

Wash mushrooms in salted water quickly, drain well.
Trim stalks at base.

Method:

Roll mushrooms in seasoned flour and then in egg wash.
Shake off surplus egg wash and roll into oatflakes.
Deep fry in hot oil at 250°-275°C until crisp and golden.
Drain on kitchen paper.
Dress into hot service dishes.

MUSHROOMS IN TOMATO AND BASIL SAUCE

Preparation:

Wash mushrooms in salted water quickly, drain well.
Trim stalks at base

Method:

Melt the butter in a thick-bottomed pan until foaming.
Add the mushrooms and sauté until light and golden.
Season with the seasoning mixture (see recipe).
Pour off any excess fat from the pan.
Deglaze with white wine.
Add the tomato and basil sauce (see recipe).
Dress into hot service dish.

OKRA

BRAISED OKRA

Preparation:

Wash in salted water, drain well.
Top and tail, cut according to the recipe.

Method:

Toss the okra in a little walnut oil.
Season with the seasoning mixture (see recipe). Pour off excess oil.
Add tomato and basil sauce (see recipe).
Braise 15-20 minutes in a moderate overn 150°-200°C.
Dress into hot service dish.

DEEP FRIED OKRA

Preparation:

Wash in salted water, drain well.
Top and tail, cut according to the recipe.

Method:

Blanch the okra in boiling salted water for 3-4 minutes.
Drain well on kitchen paper.
Roll them in seasoned flour, egg and breadcrumbs.
Deep fry in hot oil 250°-275°C until crisp and golden.
Drain on kitchen paper.
Dress into service dish and dust with paprika.

OKRA IN YOGURT

Preparation:

Wash in salted water, drain well.
Top and tail, cut according to the recipe.

Method:

Melt the butter in a thick-bottomed pan until foaming.
Add the okra and quickly toss for 2-3 minutes.
Season with the seasoning mixture (see recipe).
Pour off excess fat.
Stir in the yogurt and simmer for 10-15 minutes.
Add a hint of freshly chopped mint.
Dress in a hot service dish.

ONIONS

GLAZED BUTTON ONIONS

Preparation:

Cut the stalk end from the onion and peel away the skin.
Cut according to the recipe.

Method:

Place the onions in salted water for 5-8 minutes.
Drain well.
Melt a knob of butter in a thick-bottomed pan until foaming.
Add the onions and quickly brown in the butter.
Season with seasoning mixture (see recipe).
Dress into hot service dishes, sprinkle with chopped parsley.

STUFFED ONIONS

Preparation:

Cut the stalk end from the onion and peel away the skin.
Cut according to the recipe.

Method:

Place the onions in salted water for 5-8 minutes.
Drain well.
Cut in half crossways and remove the centre rings, leaving a shell.
Fill with stuffing mixture (see recipe).
Place into a buttered seasoned casserole.
Add a little stock, cover with a lid and braise for 30-35 minutes at 150°-200°C.
Dress into a hot service dish.

BUTTON ONION IN SAGE BATTER

Preparation:

Cut the stalk end from the onion and peel away the skin.

Method:

Place the onions in salted water for 5-8 minutes.
Drain well.
Roll in seasoned flour.
Dip into batter mixture (see recipe) with 1 teaspoon of sage per pint of batter.
Deep fry in hot oil 250°-275°C until crisp and golden.
Drain on kitchen paper.
Dress into hot service dish with a cordon of tomato and basil sauce (see recipe).

PARSNIPS

ONIONS BRAISED IN CIDER

Preparartion:

Cut the stalk end from the onion and peel away the skin,
Cut according to the recipe.

Method:

Cut onions in half and place in boiling salted water for 5-10 minutes.
Drain and place into a pan or casserole suitable for braising.
Add a mixture of ½ cider and ½ madeira sauce (see recipe) to the onions to come ⅔ of the way up the onions.
Sprinkle with chopped sage and diced apple.
Braise until tender, 20-25 minutes in a moderate oven.
Dress into a hot serving dish.

PARSNIPS BRAISED IN MADEIRA SAUCE

Preparation:

Trim the crown and root ends.
Wash well in salted water.
Prepare according to recipe.

Method:

Cut parsnips into even sized pieces.
Blanch in boiling salted water for 4-5 minutes.
Drain well and season with seasoning mixture (see recipe).
Place into a dish suitable for braising and cover ⅔ with stock.
Cover with buttered foil and braise in a moderate oven 150°-200°C for 1 hour.
Dress into a hot service dish and surround with a cordon of madeira sauce (see recipe).

HONEY BAKED PARSNIPS

Preparation:

Trim the crown and root ends.
Wash well in salted water.
Prepare according to recipe.

Method:

Cut parsnips into even sized pieces.
Place into boiling salted water for 2-3 minutes.
Drain well.
Melt beef dripping or butter into a roasting tray.
Add the parsnips and quickly seal in the hot fat.
Season with seasoning mixture (see recipe).
Pour over 1oz honey per 1lb of parsnips.
Bake in a moderate oven 150°-200°C for 45-60 minutes.
Dress into a hot service dish.

PARSNIPS IN ORANGE SAUCE

Preparation:

Trim the crown and root ends.
Wash well in salted water.
Prepare according to recipe.

Method:

Cut parsnips into even sized pieces.
Place into boiling salted water and simmer until tender.
Drain well.
Toss them in a little hot butter.
Dress into a hot service dish.
Coat with orange sauce (see recipe).

PEAS

PEPPERS

PEAS WITH BACON

Preparation:

Ready prepared deep frozen.

Method:

Melt a knob of butter in a thick-bottomed pan until foaming.
Add lardons of bacon and quickly cook.
Add cooked, refreshed petit pois.
Toss quickly together.
Season with seasoning mixture (see recipe).
Dress into service dishes.

PEAS WITH MINT

Preparation:

Ready prepared frozen

Method:

Cook the petit pois in boiling salted water for 2-3 minutes.
Refresh under cold running water.
Drain well.
Melt a knob of butter in a thick-bottomed frying pan.
Add the petit pois.
Add 1 tablespoon of chopped fresh mint per 2lb, toss quickly.
Correct seasoning with seasoning mixture (see recipe).
Dress into hot service dishes.

PEAS FRENCH STYLE

Preparation:

Ready prepared frozen

Method:

Place the petit pois into a sauteuse.
Add 1 small shredded lettuce per 2lb of petit pois and 8oz of blanched button onions.
Add a knob of butter, 1oz of sugar and season with seasoning mixture (see recipe).
Half cover with water, cover with lid and braise until tender. Correct seasoning.
Thicken with approximately 1oz of beurre manié.
Dress into hot service dish.

BATTERED PEPPER RINGS

Preparation:

Cut the stalk end off the pepper and if stuffing, cut out the seeds and membrane. If the pepper is to be sliced or diced, cut in half lengthways to scoop out the seeds more easily.

Method:

Remove seeds from 3 different coloured peppers and discard.
Cut the peppers into rings.
Dip into seasoned flour.

STIR-FRIED PEPPERS

Preparation:

Cut the stalk end off the pepper and if stuffing, cut out the seeds and membrane. If the pepper is to be sliced or diced, cut in half lengthways to scoop out the seeds more easily.

Method:

Remove seeds from 3 different coloured peppers and cut flesh into strips.
Slice 1 medium onion.
Heat a little vegetable oil in a thick-bottomed pan until a haze appears.
Add the peppers and onions.
Quickly mix together.
Season with seaoning mixture (see recipe)
Add a hint of chopped ginger and a few sesame seeds.
Dress into a hot service dish.

STUFFED PEPPERS

Preparation:

Cut the stalk end off the pepper and if stuffing, cut out the seeds and membrane. If the pepper is to be sliced or diced, cut in half lengthways to scoop out the seeds more easily.

Method:

Remove top from the peppers.
Remove seed from interior.
Fill peppers with stuffing mixture (see recipe).
Place into a suitable dish for braising.
Replace the tops onto the peppers.
1/3 cover with a good stock and cover with a lid.
Braise for 25-30 minutes in a moderate oven.
Dress into service dish.

SALSIFY

SALSIFY GLAZED

Preparation:

Scrub the salsify to remove all grit and soil.
Trim the crown and root and cut into 2 or
3 pieces 2" (5cm) long.
Place immediately in a bowl of cold water
with a little lemon juice to prevent
discoloration.

Method:

Cut the salsify into even sized pieces.
Cook in salted boiling water for 15-20
minutes.
Drain well.
Dress into a hot service dish.
Coat with cheese sauce (see recipe).
Sprinkle with a mixture of grated cheese
and white breadcrumbs.
Brown under a salamander.

SALSIFY AND HAZELNUT FRITTERS

Preparation:

Scrub the salsify to remove all grit and soil.
Trim the crown and root and cut into 2 or
3 pieces 2" (5cm) long.
Place immediately in a bowl of cold water
with a little lemon juice to prevent
discoloration.

Method:

Cut the salsify into even sized pieces.
Cook in salted boiling water for 15-20
minutes.
Drain well.
Dip each piece into flour, beaten egg and a
50-50 mixture of white breadcrumbs and
chopped hazelnuts.
Deep fry in hot oil, i.e. 250°-275°C until
crisp and golden.
Drain on kitchen paper.
Dress into hot vegetable dishes.

SALSIFY IN TOMATO AND BASIL SAUCE

Preparation:

Scrub the salsify to remove all grit and soil.
Trim the crown and root and cut into 2 or
3 pieces 2" (5cm) long.
Place immediately in a bowl of cold water
with a little lemon juice to prevent
discoloration.

Method:

Cut the salsify into even sized pieces.
Cook in salted boiling water for 15-20
minutes.
Drain well.
Dress into a hot service dish.
Coat with tomato and basil sauce (see
recipe).

SPINACH

SUBRIC OF SPINACH

Preparation:

Spinach needs patient preparation, the grit
really clings to the leaves and only several
changes of washing water will remove it,
remember the leaves damage very easily,
so they must be handled gently.
Trim the stalks.

Method:

Cook the spinach in boiling salted water.
Drain well. Purée the spinach with a little
chopped onion in a food processor.
Season with seasoning mixture (see recipe).
Add 4 eggs per pint of spinach purée and
2-3 tablespoons of cream.
Mix well and pour into buttered dariol moulds.
Poach in a bain marie 15-20 minutes.
Turn out into a vegetable dish.
Finish with a cordon of cheese sauce (see
recipe).

CREAMED SPINACH WITH BACON

Preparation:

Spinach needs patient preparation, the grit
really clings to the leaves and only several
changes of washing water will remove it,
remember the leaves damage very easily,
so they must be handled gently.
Trim the stalks.

Method:

Cook the spinach in boiling salted water.
Drain well.
Purée the spinach in a food processor.
Season with seasoning mixture (see recipe).
Add ½ pint basic white sauce (see recipe)
per 1lb of spinach purée.
Return to the heat and add 3-4 tablespoons of
double cream per 1lb. Correct the seasoning.
Dress into hot vegetable dishes.
Top with crispy lardons of bacon.

SPINACH WITH PINE KERNELS

Preparation:

Spinach needs patient preparation, the grit
really clings to the leaves and only several
changes of washing water will remove it,
remember the leaves damage very easily,
so they must be handled gently.
Trim the stalks.

Method:

Cook the spinach in boiling salted water.
Drain well.
Melt a knob of butter in a sauteuse until
foaming.
Add the pine kernels and quickly brown.
Add the leaf spinach and season with
seasoning mixture (see recipe).
Mix well to distribute the pine kernels.
Dress into hot service dishes.

TOMATO MILANAISE

Preparation:

Wash tomato in cold salted water, remove eye with a small sharp knife.

Method:

Cut tomato in half crosswise.
Season, brush with butter.
Sprinkle with parmesan cheese.
Quickly cook under a hot salamander.
Dress in a hot buttered vegetable dish.

CRISPY GARLIC TOMATOES

Preparation:

Wash tomato in cold salted water, remove eye with a small sharp knife.

Method:

Remove tops from tomato and retain for soups etc.
Season tomato with seasoning mixture (see recipe).
Top with herb and garlic mixture (see recipe).
Place onto a buttered seasoned tray.
Bake in a hot oven 200-250°C for 5-7 minutes.
Dress into a hot service dish.

STUFFED TOMATOES

Preparation:

Wash tomato in cold salted water, remove eye with a small sharp knife.

Method:

Remove tops from tomato and retain for soups etc.
Scoop the seeds from the tomato and retain for soups etc.
Fill with stuffing mixture (see recipe).
Place onto a buttered seasoned tray.
Cook slowly in the oven for 10-12 minutes.
Dress into hot service dishes.

Many vegetables are imported into Britain from numerous countries, thus lengthening the availability. The following chart shows the availability of each vegetable including whether it is British produced or imported. The main country of import is indicated by using the key provided, where more than three countries supply at any one time the symbol IMP, for imported, has been given.

	JAN	FEB	MAR	APR	MAY	JUN	JUL	AUG	SEP	OCT	NOV	DEC
Artichoke Jerusalem		UK	UK	UK	UK	UK						
Aubergine	HOLL	CYP HOLL	CYP HOLL	CYP HOLL	CYP HOLL	FR HOLL	FR HOLL	UK HOLL	UK HOLL	FR HOLL	HOLL	HOLL
Beans (Broad)				FR IT	FR IT	UK FR IT	UK FR IT	FR IT				
Beans (French)	IMP	IMP	IMP	IMP	IMP	IMP	UK IMP	UK IMP	IMP	IMP	IMP	IMP
Beans (Runner)				IMP	IMP	UK	UK	UK	UK	UK		
Broccoli	UK	UK	UK	UK	UK	IMP	IMP	IMP	IMP	UK	UK	IMP
Calabrese	IMP	IMP	IMP	IMP	UK	UK	UK	IMP	IMP	IMP	IMP	IMP
Brussels Sprouts	UK	UK	UK	UK						UK	UK	UK
Cabbage (White)	HOLL	HOLL	HOLL	HOLL	HOLL	HOLL			UK	UK	HOLL UK	HOLL
Cabbage (Red)	UK	UK	HOLL	HOLL	HOLL	HOLL			HOLL	HOLL	HOLL	UK
Carrots (New)			UK	UK	UK	UK	UK	UK				
Carrots (Old)	UK	UK	UK	UK	IMP	IMP	UK	IMP	UK	UK	UK	UK
Cauliflower	UK IMP	UK IMP	UK IMP	UK IMP	UK IMP	UK IMP	UK IMP	UK IMP	UK IMP	UK IMP	UK IMP	UK IMP
Celeriac	UK HOLL CR	HOLL FR	HOLL FR	IS	IS	IS	IS	UK	UK HOLL FR	UK HOLL FR	UK HOLL FR	UK HOLL FR
Celery	UK IS	UK IS	IS	IS	IS	UK IS	UK IS	UK IS	UK IS	UK IS	UK IS	UK IS
Chicory	BEL	BEL	BEL	BEL	BEL	BEL			BEL	BEL	BEL	BEL
Courgette	SP	SP	SP	SP FR	SP FR	UK FR	UK IT	UK IT	FR	FR	FR	SP
Fennel	IT IMP	IT IMP	IT IMP	IT IMP	IT IMP	IMP	UK BEL	UK BEL	BEL	IMP	IMP	IMP
Leeks	UK	UK	UK	UK				UK	UK	UK	UK	UK
Mange Tout	IMP	IMP	IMP	IMP	IMP	IMP	IMP	UK	UK	IMP	IMP	IMP
Marrow						UK	UK	UK	UK			
Mushrooms	UK	UK	UK	UK	UK	UK	UK	UK	UK	UK	UK	UK
Okra	KEY	KEY	KEY	KEY	KEY	KEY	KEY	KEY CYP	KEY CYP	KEY CYP	KEY CYP	KEY
Onions	UK SP	UK SP	SP	SP	SP	SP	SP	UK SP	UK	UK	UK	UK
Parsnips	UK	UK	UK	UK					UK	UK	UK	UK
Petit Pois (Frozen)	PM	PM	PM	PM	PM	PM	PM	PM	PM	PM	PM	PM
Peppers	HOLL	HOLL	HOLL	HOLL SP	HOLL SP	HOLL SP	HOLL SP	HOLL SP	HOLL	HOLL	HOLL	HOLL
Mooli	SP	SP	SP	HOLL	HOLL	HOLL	HOLL	HOLL	HOLL	HOLL	SP	SP
Salsify	BEL	BEL	BEL	BEL	BEL	BEL			BEL	BEL	BEL	BEL
Spinach	FR IT	FR IT	UK FR IT	UK FR IT	UK FR IT	UK	UK	UK	UK	UK	UK	
Sweetcorn		SP	SP	SP	SP	IMP		UK	UK	UK	UK	
Tomato	CAN SP	CAN SP	CAN	CAN	CAN UK	UK	UK	UK	UK	UK CAN SP	CAN SP	CAN SP

FR — France · HOLL — Holland · CAN — Canary Islands · USA — United States of America · IS — Israel · IT — Italy · CYP — Cyprus · KEY — Kenya · BEL — Belgium · IMP — Imported · SP — Spain · UK — United Kingdom · PM — Puritan Maid

TO CONCLUDE

SWEETS AND DESSERTS

ENVELOPES OF FRUIT

RASPBERRY CHARLOTTE

PECAN PIE

GOOSE GOG AND CARROT PIE

HAZELNUT CREAM ROLL

PLUM AND DRAMBUIE MOUSSE

DEVONSHIRE JUNKET

CRYSTALLISED CHRYSANTHEMUMS

BROWN BREAD ICE CREAM

PISTACHIO ICE CREAM

IRISH HONEY ICE CREAM

ORANGE SORBET

ROSE PETAL SORBET

ELDERFLOWER SORBET

CHAMPAGNE SORBET

HONEY WAFERS

CREME PATISSIERE

CREME ANGLAISE

WALNUT BREAD

REDCURRANT MOUSSE

PASTA FOR RAVIOLI

TRIO OF CHOCOLATE MOUSSE

TIPS:

— Pan lids clattering and banging drive me mad, so we use tin foil.
— To successfully remove mousse from metal ring moulds either use a gas touch or a hot dry knife.

"Chef Benson Smith's creations are skilfully prepared and beautifully presented, they show imagination, sensitivity and respect for quality ingredients and also reveal his enthusiastic and original interest in cooking."

SONIA ALLISON
Ideal Home Magazine

SWEETS and DESSERTS

ENVELOPES OF FRUIT
Serves Four

Dedicated to my friends at 'Castle Hill' Hospital, Cottingham

Ingredients:

12oz	Fresh Fruit (in season)
8 tbsp	Apricot Jam
2	Vanilla Pods
2 tbsp	Sugar
4 tbsp	Water
8	Mint Leaves
12	Soft Green Peppercorns

Method:

Preheat the oven to Gas Mark 7 (220°C, 425°F).
Bring the water and sugar to the boil in a saucepan. Remove from heat, add the jam and whisk lightly. Fold the sheets of tin foil into triangle shapes and place the fruits with four peppercorns and a vanilla pod, split lengthways. Top with the mint and coat with the sauce. Fold up the edges and seal. Bake in the oven for 15 to 20 minutes. Finally, serve the parcel for each guest to open.

"Thinking up new ideas and plans has always been my buzz ... a cup of tea with a scrappy bit of paper has achieved more than colleagues exploits in the local pub"
John Benson Smith

RASPBERRY CHARLOTTE
Serves Four

Ingredients:

1	Egg Yolk
15g	Castor Sugar
175ml	Raspberry Puree
1½ leaves	Gelatine (soaked in water)
85ml	Double Cream
1	Egg White
200g	Diced Raspberries (soaked in brandy)

Method:

Whisk egg yolks and 36g castor sugar to a ribbon stage. Whisk egg whites, add remaining sugar, fold whites into egg yolks one-third at a time until completely folded in. Sprinkle sieved flour into the mixture and fold in gently. Spread thinly over a greased baking tray and cook in an oven Gas Mark 7 (200°C, 400°F) for about 5 minutes. Remove from the oven and cool.

Biscuit Sponge:

4	Eggs (separated)
96g	Castor Sugar
114g	Flour

Method:

Line four 150ml souffle moulds with the biscuit sponge. Cream the egg yolk and 10g sugar. Add heated raspberry puree to the mixture and cook out.
Add soaked gelatine leaves to raspberry mixture. Cool on ice, stirring continuously. Whisk cream to the ribbon stage, add 5g of sugar, add to the mixture.
Whisk egg white to a peak, fold into the mousse, add the diced raspberries. Place the mousse into the moulds and allow to set in the refrigerator for at least 4 hours. Turn out in centre of the plate. Add a cordon of sauce anglaise. Coat with raspberry coulis and place glazed raspberry on top.

"A particular favourite of mine" **John Benson Smith**

PECAN PIE
Serves Four

Ingredients:

12 fl.oz/3½dl	Light Corn Syrup
5oz/150g	Sugar
5oz/150g	Brown Sugar
4	Whole Eggs
2	Egg Yolks
1½oz/45g	Butter
10oz/285g	Pecan Halves

Pastry Tart Tin 10 inches/25cms diameter lined with pastry dough (see below)

Sweet Paste:

1lb/500g	Flour
10oz/300g	Butter
4oz/125g	Sugar
3	Eggs

Mix the flour, butter and sugar into fine crumb, mix in the eggs and refrigerate for 1½ hours.

Chocolate Fudge Sauce:

8oz/250g	Chocolate
3 tblsp	Unsalted Butter
8oz/250g	Caster Sugar
6 tblsp	Golden Syrup
2 tblsp	Brandy
2½ fl.oz/60ml	Boiling Water

Method:

Preheat oven to Gas Mark 5 (190°C, 375°F).
In a mixing bowl, mix the corn syrup, both sugars, whole eggs and egg yolks. Mix well. In a small sauté pan, heat the butter until it turns brown and has a nutty aroma. Mix into the corn syrup mixture.
Arrange pecan halves in the bottom of the pastry lined tart shells. Ladle filling over the pecans.
Bake 40 to 45 minutes or until a skewer inserted into the pecan pie comes out clean. Cool the pie to room temperature.

Sauces which can be accompanied:

Caramel Sauce, Chocolate Fudge Sauce.

Method:

Melt the chocolate and butter, add the boiling water, stir in well. Add the sugar and golden syrup to the chocolate. Turn up the heat and bring to the boil for about 10 minutes.
Remove from the heat and cool. Stir in the brandy and refrigerate.

Hint:

A sprinkling of sugar on the surface of crème patissiere will stop the mixture from forming a crust.

GOOSE GOG AND CARROT PIE
Serves Four

Ingredients:

½kg Gooseberries
100g Grated Carrot
300g Short Paste
½-1dl Water
100g Sugar
10g Castor Sugar
Egg Wash

Method:

Prepare and wash gooseberries, place in a pan. Add the sugar and water. Cook. When cool add the carrot, mix together and place in a pie dish. Roll out pastry to approximately 3mm thick. Place a thin strip of pastry around rim of pie dish. Egg wash the strip and cover the pie with the remainder of pastry. Decorate the edge round the pie. Allow to rest for 30 minutes in a cool place, brush with egg wash and sprinkle with castor sugar. Place in the oven at 215°C until lightly brown (approximately 15 minutes), reduce temperature to approximately 190°C and allow to cook for a further 30 minutes.

'British Food, a rustic style of regional specialities collected together, form a view of our ancestral cooking.
These old ideas and beliefs have been incorporated into the modern style. We are what we eat — Good, Strong and Traditional"
Nigel Wright, Sous Chef from Lancashire

HAZELNUT CREAM ROLL
Serves Six

Ingredients:

3 Eggs
3oz Castor Sugar
3oz Ground Hazelnuts
2 Level tablespoons Wholemeal Flour
1 fl.oz Whipping Cream
8oz Blackberries

Method:

Whisk eggs and sugar over a bain marie until thick and pale (approximately 10 minutes). Remove from the heat and fold in hazelnuts. Cook until golden.
Evenly cover with whipped cream and blackberries.
Roll out and freeze for ½ hour to keep the shape.
Slice, using an electric carving knife, and lay on a bed of fruit purée.

PLUM AND DRAMBUIE MOUSSE
Serves Six

Ingredients:

6 Eggs (size 4, brown)
½oz/15g 1 tablespoon Gelatine
4oz/115g Castor Sugar
½pt/3dl Plum Puree
1oz/¼dl Drambuie
1pt/6dl Whipped Cream
6-8 Fresh Plums
6-8 Mint Leaves

Method:

Separate the eggs and beat the whites until stiff.
Dissolve the gelatine in a small amount of water, beat the yolks and add sugar. Fold in the plum puree and drambuie. Add the gelatine and fold in the egg whites. Refrigerate.

Serve in individual ramakins. Garnish with the plums and fresh cream.

"The pastry chef's face when he discovered 'Benson Smith the apprentice' had just chopped garlic on his work top where a hundred flans were standing"
John Benson Smith

DEVONSHIRE JUNKET

Serves Four

Junket sets at room temperature — no draughts please

Ingredients:

1 pt Milk
1 Desertspoon Sugar
2 Tablespoons Brandy
1 Teaspoon Rennet
4oz Clotted Cream
Cinnamon or Nutmeg
Little Cream

Method:

Bring milk to blood heat.
Mix in a bowl with sugar and brandy.
Stir slowly and add the Rennet essence
(stirring too much will cause bubbles).
Pour into dishes and set at room
temperature for 30 mins.
Pour a little cream on top, and top with
nutmeg.
Serve with clotted cream.

CRYSTALLISED CHRYSANTHEMUMS

Serves Four

See Cooking with Flowers

Ingredients:

4 Yellow Chrysanthemums
4oz/115g Castor Sugar (liquidised)
1 Egg White
Pinch of Salt
Juice of ½ Lemon
4oz/115g Strawberries
1½ dl Syrup
4 Kiwi Fruit
4oz/1 dl Double Cream

Note:

Flowers must be fresh and not sprayed by
insecticides or chemicals

Method:

Remove the stalks of the flower, cut off
close to the flower. Wash the flowers
ensuring no flies are inside the petals.
Slightly beat the egg whites with the pinch
of salt and the lemon juice, result should be
watery.
Completely coat each flower with the egg
white ensuring no gaps. Snake off any
excess white and stand to drain for a few
seconds. Completely cover the flowers in
the sugar, all patches must be covered,
leave to dry on a wire rack for 8 to 24
hours.
Liquidise the strawberries with a little sugar
syrup and strain.
Peel and slice the kiwi fruit.
Whip the cream, place the kiwi slices
around in the centre of the plate layered
with the whipped cream. Pour the
strawberry puree around the base. Place a
flower in the centre of each plate and
serve.

---

*"I can tell from the canapés at Friday night's peach champagne cocktails that we're in for
a culinary thrill from young Chef de Cuisine John Benson Smith"*
London Weekend Standard

AS A TRAINEE:
*"Whoever was my senior, my aim was always within six months to be quicker, cleaner
and better at all times and without the mouth or attitude problem"*
John Benson Smith

ICE CREAM AND SORBETS

Note: When making ice creams and sorbets, a machine is more convenient and a lot less hassle!

BROWN BREAD ICE CREAM
Serves Six

Ingredients:

4oz/100g Brown Bread
4oz/100g Sugar
1/2pt/100 fl.oz/300ml Double Cream
2 Eggs
1 tsp Vanilla Essence

Method:

Blend the bread in a food processor until you have a fine crumb. Mix the crumbs with 1oz of the sugar and put on a baking tray in a hot oven Gas Mark 6 (200°C,400°F) until they are browned. You may need to turn them once or twice.

Separate the eggs, beat the yolks and the sugar together and, beating continuously, pour over the cream which has been heated to just below boiling point. Pour the mixture back into a saucepan and then heat gently, stirring constantly until the **mixture thickens enough to coat the back** of the spoon. **Do not boil.**

Stir in the vanilla essence, the cooked breadcrumbs and finally whip the egg whites and fold into the mix.

Freeze in an ice cream machine or make by hand.

PISTACHIO ICE CREAM
Serves Six

Ingredients:

4 Egg Yolks
3oz/75g Sugar
1/2pt/10 fl.oz/300ml Milk
1/2pt/10 fl.oz/300ml Double Cream
4oz/100g Pistachio Nuts
1 tsp Almond Essence

Method:

Bring a pan of water to the boil, drop in the pistachio nuts and leave for two minutes. Drain and skin and roughly chop the nuts.

Use the egg yolks, sugar and milk to make a crème anglaise (see notes). Rapidly cool the crème anglaise. Mix in the double cream, pistachio nuts and the almond essence. Pour the mixture into an ice cream maker or if one is not available, freeze. Using a plastic spatula stir every ten minutes until frozen.

IRISH HONEY ICE CREAM
Serves Six (Makes Half Gallon)

Ingredients:

6 Eggs (separated)
1/2pt/300g Clear Honey
5 fl.oz/1/4pt/150ml Baileys Irish Cream Liqueur
1/2pt/300g Whipped Double Cream
8oz/200g Icing Sugar

Method:

Beat the egg yolks until thick.
Whisk whites until stiff.
Fold together.
Add the cream, honey, liqueur and sugar.
Freeze for 6 hours, turning the mix every 30 minutes until frozen.

Ice Cream Sorbet

ORANGE SORBET
Serves Six

Ingredients:

8oz/225g Granulated Sugar
1pt/600g Water
½pt/10 fl.oz/300g Fresh Orange Juice
Juice of 1 Lemon
Zest of 2 Oranges

Method:

Put the sugar and water into a saucepan and stir over a gentle heat until the sugar has dissolved. Bring to the boil for about 8 minutes, or until you have a light syrup (approximately 115°C, 230°F).

Leave until it is at room temperature and then stir in the lemon juice, orange juice and orange zest. Pour into a sorbet machine or make by hand.

ROSE PETAL SORBET
Serves Six

Ingredients:

½pt/275ml Water
8oz/225g Castor Sugar
Petals from 6 large red/pink scented roses (fresh, not chemically sprayed)
Juice from 2 Lemons
½pt/275ml White English Wine

Rosewater essence could be appropriate in winter

Method:

Boil the water and sugar to form a syrup. Skim and cool for 10 minutes. Chop the rose petals in a food processor and add to the syrup.
Add the lemon juice and wine to the syrup, leave for 15 minutes.
Pass through a strainer and skim. Taste. If necessary add a few drops of essence.
Freeze until mushy, whisk every 10 minutes preventing the sorbet from freezing too quickly.
When hard cover and store.

To Serve:

Remove from the freezer and defrost 20 minutes before serving.
Decorate and garnish.

ELDERFLOWER SORBET
Serves Six

Ingredients:

Zest of 1 Lemon
¾pt/450ml Fresh Lemon Juice
7oz/175g Sugar
1¼pt/750ml Cold Water
6 Large Elderflower Heads
2 Egg Whites

Method:

Add lemon juice, lemon zest and sugar to the water, submerge the elderflower heads in the liquid and bring to the boil.

Leave to cool and infuse, then strain off the flower heads and either transfer to an ice cream maker or constantly stir until half frozen. Whip the egg whites and fold into the sorbet before the sorbet freezes completely.

Advice:

Having equipment to hand is vital for a successful recipe.

CHAMPAGNE SORBET
Serves Four

Ingredients:

7oz/200g Sugar
12 fl.oz/350ml Water
½pt/300ml Cream
Juice of 2 Lemons
Half Bottle Champagne

Method:

Put the sugar and water in a saucepan, bring slowly to the boil then turn up the heat and boil for about 5 minutes until you have a light syrup (it is best to use a sugar thermometer until the temperature 115°C, 230°F is reached). Take the syrup off the heat and leave it until it is cool. Mix in the champagne, cream and lemon juice. Pour mixture into a sorbet machine or make by hand.

"Dinner conversation over rose petal sorbet, seafood terrine and a dessert trolley that makes Babette's feast seem frugal fare, is of caged ducks in Bangkok, of pigs riding pillion in Nigeria, of puddings rising high in Yorkshire (add an egg white for every egg, says Chef").
London Evening Standard

BASIC RECIPES

HONEY WAFERS

Ingredients:

14oz/400g Icing Sugar
14oz/400g Flour
10oz/300g Butter (soft)
10oz/300g Clear Honey
       10 Egg Whites

Method:

Sift the sugar and flour and rub in the softened butter. Pour the honey into the mixture. Mix the egg whites into the mixture and refrigerate.

To cook:

Using a template (a design of your own creation), spread the paste thinly on a greased baking tray using a palette knife. Cook at 200°C until brown.

Slide the wafer off the tray and mould while the biscuit is still warm into the desired shape.

Advice:

Weigh out and measure all the ingredients before commencing the recipe.

CREME PATISSIERE

Ingredients:

2pts Milk
   7 Eggs
3oz/100g Flour
4oz/125g Sugar

Method:

Boil the milk.
Whisk the eggs, sugar and flour.
Pour the boiling milk onto the paste.
Return to a clean pan and return to the heat until thickened. Refrigerate.

CREME ANGLAISE

Ingredients:

1 pt Milk
1 pt Whipping Cream
   8 Egg Yolks
4oz/125g Sugar

Method:

Boil the milk and the whipping cream.
Whisk the egg yolks and sugar.
Pour the boiling milk and cream onto the egg mixture and whisk.
Add vanilla essence if necessary.
Simmer for 10 mins.
Pour into a clean container and refrigerate.

WALNUT BREAD
Makes Two 2lb (1kg) Loaves

Recommended to serve the bread as an accompaniment with cheese after a meal. The bread has an interesting texture and flavour.

Ingredients:

1lb 12oz/800g Strong Plain Flour
1½ level tsp Salt
   1 sachet Harvest Gold Dried Yeast
   3oz/75g Light Brown Soft Sugar
   4oz/125g Chopped Walnuts
   ¾pt/430ml Warm Milk
   4 tbsp Warm Water
        1 Beaten Egg (for brushing)

Method:

Sift flour and salt into a bowl, mix in the yeast, sugar and walnuts. Mix into a dough with the warm milk and water.
Turn out onto a floured surface and knead for 10 minutes until smooth. Return to a buttered bowl, cover with a damp cloth and leave in a warm place until it doubles in size.
Re-knead quickly and cut into 2 pieces. Shape into greased loaf tins. Leave again until is rises. Brush the top with the egg and bake for 10 minutes at Gas Mark 8 (230°C, 450°F), reduce to Gas Mark 4 (180°C, 350°F) for 20 minutes, then turn out onto wire racks to cool.

REDCURRANT MOUSSE
Serves Four

Ingredients:

280g Redcurrants (fresh)
4oz/230g Sugar
4 Egg Yolks
10g Powdered Gelatine
2 tsp Creme de Cassis Liqueur
¼pt/140ml Double Cream (lightly whipped)

Redcurrant Jelly:

4oz/110g Sugar
6oz/170g Redcurrants
2 tsp Powdered Gelatine

Method:

Put the redcurrants and sugar in a pan and boil. Liquidise. Whisk the egg yolks and pour the liquidised purée onto the yolks. Dissolve the gelatine in two teaspoons of water, add this to the mousse mixture while still warm. Whisk until a mousse is obtained. Add the liqueur. Fill an 8 inch or 20cm flan ring and leave to set in the refrigerator.

Redcurrant Jelly:

Dissolve the sugar in 8 fl.oz/230ml of water. Boil the remaining redcurrants. Liquidise and allow to cool. Dissolve ¼pt/140ml of the purée into the gelatine. Spread over the set mousse. Leave in the refrigerator for 2-3 hours.

Serve with the mousse the remaining **purée and the whipped cream.**

PASTA FOR RAVIOLI

Basic Dough Ingredients:

9oz/250g Medium Strength Plain White Flour
5 Egg Yolks
2 Pinch Salt
2 tblsp Olive Oil
1-2 tblsp Water

Method:

Put all the ingredients in the given order into a food processor and mix for 30 seconds until blended. Knead the dough until smooth, wrap in cling film and rest for one hour.

Divide pasta dough in half. Flatten into rectangles, stretch and roll out as thinly as possible, leave to rest for two minutes.

Place a teaspoon of filling in one half and brush other half with water, seal edges.

Cut and seal. Freeze for 30 minutes. Cook in full boiling chicken stock with tarragon and salt for 1-2 minutes.

"My first ever cookery demonstration — in Sussex — I was so nervous my knives clattered — I looked around for a window — a smiling lady so big she blocked out the sunlight — blocked my escape"
John Benson Smith

TRIO OF CHOCOLATE MOUSSE
To make One Terrine (8 portions)

This is the recipe for one Chocolate Mousse. Repeat three times using three different colours.

Ingredients:

⅓ of Pint **Crème Anglaise**
(see recipe)
3oz Chocolate
1 leaf Gelatine
¾ of Pint Whipped Cream

Method:

Make Crème Anglaise.
Add the melted chocolate and the soaked gelatine. Pass through a Chinois and cool until setting point. Fold in whipped cream. Leave to set before proceeding with the other layers.

Trio of Chocolate Mousse

TO COMPLETE

STOCKS AND SAUCES

BROWN/WHITE STOCK

FISH STOCK

CHICKEN STOCK

ROUX

BASIC WHITE/BROWN SAUCE

VELOUTE

ROAST GRAVY

HOLLANDAISE

SAUCE RECIPES

"Building cannot be safe without basic and firm foundations,

these are just that, basic"

John Benson Smith

Looking back at the end of my school days, the choice of careers seemed endless, so why on earth did I have to choose a life which gives you long, difficult and strenuous hours from early in the morning until late at night. Having the Chef pushing the last fragment of energy from your body and soul, and still wanting more. The sheer hell of the pressure, the hot stoves, the burning pans, the cold fridges and the nagging waiters!

The reason, probably, the grit and determination that all chefs have, gave me a good start (I hate giving up) and the enjoyment of doing something completely different from what I have been accustomed to.

Being a Chef, and a Patissiere Chef at that, gives you the main ingredient of life, the power to control your emotions in those tight situations and come out alive and kicking. The feeling you receive within yourself to create a dish from nothing, the source of imagination sparks up and the desire to go where others have not trod bursts into flower to make that deliberate statement of your overwhelming passion of food, those last touches, the sprig of fresh mint, the cordon of sauce.

I would like to think of myself as a parachute 'dare devil' who tries, after landing on his feet the first time, edging further up into the sky to see if it is possible to obtain the same feat. A Chef is similar but, thank heavens, a little safer in his work. The same drive, ambition and determination links the two, each have their barriers to be broken.

Pastry is set in a class of its own, not because its Chefs have better talent or professionalism, but because their strength lies in different areas. They have different products to use, chocolate instead of salad, fruit instead of meat and so on, but still there is that subtle and suggestive rivalry between the brigade.

I hope you enjoy the compilations of our recipes, and remember Patissiere is

"An Affair of the Heart".

ADAM RICHARDSON

STOCKS

STOCKS

Stock is a liquid containing some of the soluble nutrients and flavours of food which are extracted by prolonged and gentle simmering (with the exception of fish stock) which requires only 20 minutes; such liquid is the foundation of soups, sauces and gravies.

Stocks are the foundation of many important kitchen preparations, therefore the greatest possible care should be taken in their preparation.

DO'S and DON'TS:

1 Bad meat or bones and decaying vegetables will give stock an unpleasant flavour and cause it to deteriorate very quickly.

2 Scum should be removed, otherwise it will boil into the stock and spoil the colour and flavour quickly.

3 Fat should be skimmed, otherwise it will taste greasy.

4 Stock should always simmer gently, for if it is allowed to boil quickly, it will evaporate and go cloudy.

5 It should not be allowed to go off the boil, otherwise, in hot weather, there is a danger of it going sour and fermenting.

6 When making Chicken Stock, if raw bones are not available, roast bones should be used.

7 If stock is to be kept, strain, re-boil, cool quickly and place in the refrigerator immediately.

THE STOCKS

White Beef Stock
White Mutton Stock
White Veal Stock
White Chicken Stock

Uses of the above:

White Soups, Sauces and Stews.

THE STOCKS:

Brown Beef Stock
Brown Mutton Stock
Brown Veal Stock
Brown Chicken Stock
Brown Game Stock

Uses of the above:

Brown Soups, Sauces, Gravies and Stews.

General Proportions of Ingredients for all stock:

1 gal/4 litre Water
4lb/2kg Raw Bones
1lb/½kg Vegetables (onion, carrot, celery, leek)

General Method for all White Stocks (except fish stock):

Chop up bones, remove any fat or marrow. Place in a stock pot, add the cold water and bring to the boil. If the scum is dirty then blanch and wash off the bones, re-cover with cold water and re-boil. Skim, wipe round sides of the pot and simmer gently. Add the washed, peeled, whole vegetables. Simmer for 6-8 hours. Skim and strain.

During the cooking a certain amount of evaporation must take place, therefore add 1 pt (½ litre) cold water just before boiling point is reached. This will also help to throw the scum to the surface and make it easier to skim.

General Method for all Brown Stocks:

Chop the bones and brown well on all sides either by:
a) placing a roasting tin in the oven, or
b) carefully browning in a little fat in a frying pan.

Drain off any fat and place the bones in stock pot. Brown any sediment that may be in the bottom of the tray, deglaze (swill out) with 1pt (½ litre) of boiling water, simmer for a few minutes and add to the bones. Add the cold water, bring to the boil and skim. Wash, peel and roughly cut the vegetables, fry in a little fat until brown, strain and add to the bones. Simmer for 6-9 hours. Skim and strain.

For brown stock a few squashed tomatoes and washed mushroom trimmings may also be added to improve the flavour.

FISH STOCK

Ingredients:

1 gal/4 litre	Cold Water	
	4lb/2kg	White Bones (Sole or Turbot)
	8oz/200g	Onion
	2oz/50g	Butter
	1 bottle	White Wine
		Parsley Stalks

Method:

Melt the butter in a thick bottomed pan.
Add the sliced onions, the well-washed fish
bones and the remainder of the ingredients.
Cover with greaseproof paper and a lid and
sweat for 5 minutes. Remove greaseproof
paper.
Add the water, bring to the boil, skim and
simmer for 20 minutes, then strain.
If the fish stock is allowed to cook for
longer than 20 minutes the flavour is not
improved, and may be spoiled.

CHICKEN STOCK

Ingredients:

1 gal/4 litre	Water	
	4lb/2kg	Chicken Bones
	1lb/½kg	Vegetables
		(Onion, Celery, Leek)

**General Method for all White Stocks
(except fish stock):**

Chop up the bones, remove any fat or
marrow.
Place in a stock pot, add the cold water
and bring to the boil.
If the scum is dirty then blanch and wash
off the bones, re-cover with cold water and
re-boil.
Skim, wipe round sides of the pot and
simmer gently.
Add the washed, peeled, whole vegetables.
Simmer for 6-8 hours.
Skim and strain.

During the cooking a certain amount of
evaporation must take place, therefore add
1 pint (½ litre) cold water just before
boiling point is reached. This will also help
to throw scum to the surface and make it
easier to skim.

*"Three weeks as an apprentice. I tripped up with sixty portions of Coq au Vin outside the
Function Room. The Chef just glared, he didn't say a word"*
John Benson Smith

SAUCES

A sauce is a liquid which has been thickened by
a) roux
b) cornflour, arrowroot or fecule
c) beurre manie (kneaded butter)
d) egg yolks

All sauces should be smooth, glossy in appearance, definite in taste and light in texture, that is to say the thickening medium should be used in moderation.

The Roux:

A roux is a combination of fat and flour which are cooked together. There are three degrees to which a roux may be cooked, namely: White Roux, Blond Roux, Brown Roux

A boiling liquid should never be added to a hot roux as the result may be lumpy and the person making the sauce may be scalded by the steam produced. If allowed to stand for a time over a moderate heat a sauce made with a roux may become thin due to chemical change (dextrinisation) in the flour.

White Roux

Uses: bechamel sauce (white sauce), soups.

Equal quantities of butter and flour cooked together without colouring for a few minutes to a sandy texture.

Blond Roux

Uses: veloutes, tomato sauce, soups.

Equal quantities of butter and flour cooked for a little longer than a white roux but without colouring to a sandy texture.

Brown Roux

Uses: espagnole (brown sauce), soups.

  8oz/200g Dripping to
10oz/250g Flour per
1 gal/4 litre Stock

Cooked together slowly to a light-brown colour. Overcooking of brown roux causes the starch to change chemically (dextrinise) and lose some of its thickening property. This will cause the fat to separate from the roux and rise to the surface of the soup or sauce being made. It will also cause too much roux to be used to achieve the required thickness and will give an unpleasant flavour.

Other Thickening Agents for Sauces: Cornflour, Arrowroot or Fecule

Uses: jus-lie and sauces

These are diluted with water, stock or milk, then stirred into the boiling liquid and allowed to re-boil for a few minutes.

Beurre manie

Uses: chiefly fish sauces

Equal quantities of butter and flour kneaded to a smooth paste and mixed into a boiling liquid.

Egg Yolks

Uses: mayonnaise, hollandaise and custard sauces

Refer to the appropriate recipe as the egg yolks are used in a different manner for each sauce.

BASIC SAUCE RECIPES
One Quart (One Litre)

Basic Sauces:

Bechamel, veloute, espagnole, demi-glace, sauce tomate, sauce hollandaise

White Sauce 1 quart (1 litre)

This is the basic white sauce made from milk and white roux.

Ingredients:

1 quart/1 litre Milk
     4oz/100g Butter
     4oz/100g Flour
            1 Onion (studded)

Method:

Melt the butter in a thick bottomed pan.
Add the flour and mix in.
Cook for a few minutes over a gentle heat without colouring.
Gradually add the warmed milk and stir until smooth.
Add the onion studded with a clove.
Allow to simmer for 30 minutes.
Remove the onion, pass the sauce through a conical strainer.
Cover with film or butter to prevent a skin forming.

"The days of overweight, fat, crackers, crazy screaming chefs in dark dirty kitchens is over — well nearly!"
John Benson Smith

BROWN SAUCE
One Quart (One Litre)

Ingredients:

2oz/50g	Good Dripping
2½oz/60g	Flour
1 quart/1 litre	Brown Stock
1oz/25g	Tomato Puree
4oz/100g	Carrot
4oz/100g	Onion

Method:

Melt the dripping in a thick bottomed pan.
Add the flour, cook out slowly to a light
brown colour, stirring frequently.
Cool and mix into the tomato purée.
Gradually mix in the boiling stock.
Bring to the boil.
Wash, peel and roughly cut the carrots and
onions.
Lightly brown in a little fat in a frying pan.
Drain off the fat and add to the sauce.
Simmer gently for 4-6 hours.
Skim when necessary. Strain.

Care should be taken when making the
brown roux not to allow it to cook too
quickly, otherwise the starch in the flour
(which is the thickening agent) will burn,
and its thickening properties weaken.

Over browning should also be avoided as
this tends to make the sauce taste bitter.

VELOUTE (Chicken, Veal, Fish, Mutton)
One Quart (One Litre)

This is a basic white sauce made from white stock and a blond roux.

Ingredients:

4oz/100g	Butter
4oz/100g	Flour
1 quart/1 litre	Stock (chicken, veal, fish, mutton) as required

Method:

Melt the butter in a thick bottomed pan.
Add the flour and mix in.
Cook out to a sandy texture over gentle
heat without colour.
Allow the roux to cool.
Gradually add the boiling stock.
Stir until smooth and boiling.
Allow to simmer approximately 1 hour.
Pass through a fine conical strainer.

A veloute sauce for chicken, veal or fish
dishes is usually finished with cream, and in
some cases, egg yolks.

DEMI-GLACE SAUCE
One Quart (One Litre)

This is a refined espagnole and is made by simmering 1 quart (1 litre) espagnole and 1 quart
(1 litre) brown stock and reducing by half. Skim off all impurities as they rise to the surface
during cooking. Pass through a fine chinoise (conical strainer), re-boil, correct the seasoning.

ROAST GRAVY
Half Pint (Quarter Litre)
Serves 4 - 6

Ingredients:

8oz/200g Raw Bones
2oz/50g Onion
1oz/25g Celery
2oz/50g Carrot
1pt/250ml Stock or Water

For preference use beef bones for roast beef gravy and the appropriate bones for lamb, veal, mutton and pork.

Method:

Chop bones and brown in the oven or brown in a little fat on top of the stove in a frying pan.
Drain off all fat.
Place in a saucepan with the stock or water.
Bring to the boil, skim and allow to simmer.
Add the lightly browned mirepoix which may be fried a little in a frying pan, or added to the bones when partly browned.
Simmer for 1½-2 hours.

Remove the joint from the roasting tin when cooked.
Return the tray to a low heat to allow the sediment to settle.
Carefully strain off the fat, leaving the sediment in the tin.
Return to the stove and brown carefully, swill (deglace) with the brown stock.
Allow to simmer for a few minutes.
Correct the colour and seasoning.
Strain and skim.

HOLLANDAISE SAUCE
Half Pint (Quarter Litre)
Serves 4 - 6

Ingredients:

8oz/200g Butter
          Salt, Cayenne
2 Egg Yolks

Method:

Mix in the yolks with a whisk.
Return to a gentle heat and whisking continuously cook to a sabayon (this is the cooking of the yolks to a thickened consistency, like cream, sufficient to show the mark of the whisk). Remove from heat and cool slightly. Whisk in gradually the melted warm butter until thoroughly combined. Correct the seasoning.
Pass through a muslin, tammy cloth, or fine chinois.
The sauce should be kept at only a slightly warm temperature until served.
Serve in a slightly warm sauceboat.

The cause of hollandaise curdling is either because the butter has been added too quickly, or because of excess heat, which will cause the albumen in the eggs to harden, shrink and separate from the liquid.

Should the sauce curdle, place a teaspoon of boiling water in a clean sauteuse and gradually whisk in the egg yolk.
Whisk lightly over gentle heat until slightly thickened. Remove from heat and gradually add the curdled sauce whisking continuously.

Served with hot fish (salmon, trout, turbot) and vegetables (asparagus, cauliflower).

AS A TRAINEE:
"My hands were so full of cuts and blue plasters as an apprentice, my father thought I was wearing gloves"
John Benson Smith

BASIC WHITE SAUCE *(1 litre)*

Ingredients:

1qt/1 litre Milk
4oz/100g Butter
4oz/100g Flour
1 Studded Onion

Method:

Melt the butter in a thick bottomed pan.
Add the flour and mix in well.
Cook for a few minutes over a gentle heat
without colouring.
Gradually add the warmed milk and stir
until smooth.
Add the onion studded with a clove.
Allow to simmer for 20 minutes.
Remove onion as pass.

LEMON SAUCE

Ingredients:

1qt/1 litre Basic White Sauce
2 Lemons (zest only)
Salt and Pepper to taste

Method:

Cut the zest into thin strips, pour in enough
water to cover, cook until tender.
Boil the basic white sauce, remove from heat,
add lemon zest and cooking liquor, simmer
sauce for 5 minutes, do not pass, season to
taste.

CHEESE SAUCE

Ingredients:

1qt/1 litre Basic White Sauce
8oz/100g Grated Cheddar Cheese
Salt and Pepper to taste

Method:

Mix well in boiling sauce, remove from the
heat.
Strain if necessary but do not allow to boil
again.

DILL SAUCE

Ingredients:

1qt/1 litre Basic White Sauce
1 tbsp Dried or Fresh Dill
Salt and Pepper to taste

Method:

Boil Cream Sauce, remove from the heat.
Add the dill to the sauce and simmer for
4-5 minutes, season to taste.

ORANGE SAUCE

Ingredients:

1qt/1 litre Basic White Sauce
2 Oranges (zest only)

Method:

Bring the sauce to the boil, remove from
the heat.
Cut the orange zest into thin strips, pour in
enough water to cover, cook until tender.
Add the zest and cooking liquid to sauce,
simmer for 8-10 minutes, season to taste.

CAPER SAUCE

Ingredients:

1qt/1 litre Basic White Sauce
4 tbsp Chopped Capers
Salt and Pepper to taste

Method:

Add the capers to the boiling sauce,
remove from the heat — season to taste,
do not allow sauce to re-boil.

CREAM SAUCE

Ingredients:

1qt/1 litre Basic White Sauce
Whipping Cream
Salt and Pepper to taste

Method:

Bring the sauce to the boil, remove from
the heat, add cream to the sauce to give
the consistency of double cream.

GREEN PEPPERCORN SAUCE

Ingredients:

1qt/1 litre	Basic White Sauce
½ tin	Soft Green Peppercorns
	Salt and Pepper to taste

Method:

Bring the sauce to the boil, remove from the heat, add peppercorns, allow to simmer for 10 minutes, season to taste.

PARSLEY SAUCE

Ingredients:

1qt/1 litre	Basic White Sauce
2 tbsp	Chopped Parsley
	Salt and Pepper to taste

Method:

Bring the sauce to the boil, remove from the heat, add the parsley to the sauce, season to taste, enrich with cream if desired.

MUSTARD SAUCE

Ingredients:

1qt/1 litre	Basic White Sauce
4 tbsp	Whole Grain Mustard
	Salt and Pepper to taste

Method:

Bring the sauce to the boil, remove from the heat, and whisk the mustard into the sauce, place back on the heat and simmer for 10 minutes. Season to taste.

MADEIRA SAUCE

Ingredients:

1qt/1 litre	Demi Glace
8 tbsp	Madeira Wine
4oz/100g	Butter
	Salt and Pepper to taste

Method:

Bring the demi glace to the boil
Add the madeira, re-boil. Correct the seasoning. Pass through a fine sieve.
Slowly mix in the butter, do not re-boil.

TOMATO AND BASIL SAUCE

Ingredients:

4oz/100g	Finely chopped Onion or Shallot
1 clove	Crushed Garlic
1oz/30g	Dried or Fresh Basil
8oz/240g	Butter
2/5 pt/200ml	Olive Oil
3lb/1150g	Tomato Concasse
½pt/250ml	White Wine

Method:

Sweat the shallots/onions and garlic in oil.
Add the wine and make reduction.
Add the tomato concasse and basil.
Cook for approximately 15 minutes on low heat.
Blend in the butter, season to taste, do not pass.

ITALIAN SAUCE

Ingredients:

8oz/200g	Chopped Mushrooms
2oz/40g	Chopped Shallots or Onions
2oz/100g	Butter
4oz/100g	Chopped lean Ham
1lb/400g	Tomato Concasse
1qt/1000ml	Demi-glace
	Chopped Parsley, Chervil and Tarragon

Method:

Melt the butter in thick-bottomed pan.
Add the shallots and gently cook for 2-3 minutes.
Add the mushrooms and gently cook for 4-5 minutes.
Add remaining ingredients, correct the seasoning, simmer for 8-10 minutes.

HERB AND GARLIC MIXTURE

Ingredients:

8oz/200g	Butter
4oz/100g	White Breadcrumbs
1oz/25g	Chopped Garlic
1oz/25g	Chopped Parsley
½oz/10g	Seasoning Mixture

Method:

Melt the butter in a thick-bottomed pan.
Add chopped garlic and sweat lightly.
Add white breadcrumbs, chopped parsley and seasoning, mix well.
Allow to cool, use as required.

VEGETABLE STUFFING

Ingredients:

6oz Cooked Wild Rice (Uncle Bens)
4oz Carrot (cut into ¼" dice)
4oz Green of Leeks or Spring Onion
    (cut into ¼" dice)
4oz Diced Onion
4oz Sultanas
4oz Buckwheat
½ tsp Grated Nutmeg
½ tsp Ground Ginger
1 Egg
4oz Fresh White Breadcrumbs
    Salt and Pepper to taste
2oz Vegetable Oil

Method:

Sweat the carrot, onions and leek in butter until glazed.
Mix all ingredients together, then bind with the egg, allow to rest for 15 minutes before using.

Note:

This stuffing is suitable for vegetarian dishes.

SEASONING MIXTURE

Ingredients:

1lb/500g Salt
1oz/25g Ground White Pepper
1oz/25g Ground Nutmeg
½ tsp Cayenne Pepper

Method:

Mix thoroughly together.
Store in air-tight container.

BATTER MIXTURE

Ingredients:

1lb/400g Flour
1oz/25g Yeast
1pt/500ml Water or Milk
    Salt and Pepper to taste

Method:

Sift the flour and salt into a basin.
Dissolve the yeast in a little of the water/milk.
Make a well in the flour.
Add the yeast and the liquid.
Gradually incorporate the flour and beat to a smooth mixture.
Allow to rest for 1 hour before using.

BATTER MIXTURE

Ingredients:

1lb/400g Flour
1 Egg
    Salt to taste
1pt/500ml Water or Milk
2 tbsp Oil

Method:

Sift the flour and salt into a basin.
Make a well.
Add the egg and the liquid.
Gradually incorporate the flour, beat to a smooth mixture.
Mix in the oil.
Allow to rest before using.

POLONAISE MIXTURE

Ingredients:

12oz/350g Fresh White Breadcrumbs
2lb/1000g Butter
4 Sieved hard boiled Eggs

Method:

Heat the butter, add the breadcrumbs in a frying pan and lightly brown, add eggs.

"I wonder if my apprentices realise they will be competing directly against me in ten-fifteen years time, in different hotels and restaurants as head chefs" **JBS**

Metric Conversion Scale and Oven Temperatures

Delivery and Storage

Liquids:

Imperial	Recommended 'ml'
¼ pint	150ml
½ pint	300ml
¾ pint	450ml
1 pint	600ml
1½ pint	900ml
1¾ pint	1 litre

Solids:

Imperial	Recommended 'g'
1oz	25g
2oz	50g
4oz	100g
8oz	225g
12oz	350g
14oz	400g
16oz	450g
2.2lb	1 kg

Oven Temperatures:

Celsius °C	Fahrenheit °F	Gas	Temperature
110°C	225°F	¼	Very Cool
130°C	250°F	½	Very Cool
140°C	275°F	1	Cool
150°C	300°F	2	Cool
170°C	325°F	3	Warm
180°C	350°F	4	Moderate
190°C	375°F	5	Fairly Hot
200°C	400°F	6	Fairly Hot
220°C	425°F	7	Hot
230°C	450°F	8	Very Hot
240°C	475°F	9	Very Hot

"The standard of cooking is high in this elegant restaurant" — *Black Swan.*
Egon Ronay Guide to Healthy Eating Out

The fundamental importance of these two areas cannot be emphasised enough. Accepting only 100% A1 quality produce into the kitchen is paramount.

Ordering food is easy, it is only forward planning and experience ... a gut feeling of business trends helps.

A firm hand is required when accepting deliveries. Constant supervision ensures suppliers only leave you with the freshest 100% top quality A1 condition goods.

A busy schedule of deliveries greets most drivers, and we are not exactly on any beaten track, he is irrate from a long drive and eager to be on his way, but you must state you are not going to accept, let's say, a couple of less than perfect items and wish replacements on credit notes. Only by this kind of firm solid action will the high standard of your requirements be impressed, implanted and remembered by suppliers.

Luckily these situations seldom occur and I receive only firm tomatoes 'red', thin crispy asparagus 'green', and 'orange' oranges, fish as sweet as though we were a seaport and meat lean and hung as I want.

Storing food properly is the only way to ensure you keep your 'quality' in tip top condition.

Refrigerate everything immediately upon arrival.

Never mix raw and cooked and segregate all foods from each other in these specified areas.

Wash all vegetables and fruits in a weak solution of water and chlorine tablets.

First and foremost keep all areas scrupulously clean, hygiene in the kitchen along with safe working procedures is number one in any kitchen.

John Benson Smith

Cooking with FLOWERS

A few words of advice ....
Original 'Olde English' recipes and medications used to incorporate flowers. Like all fashions in foods, use diminished and has slowly and quietly been revived. Used for many centuries as flavourings and colourings, care has obviously to be taken when cooking with flowers. As a rule, discard stalks, roots, stems and stamens and treat the flowers gently. The Chinese were the first people on record to use flowers in 3000 BC. After the downfall of the Roman Empire their use declined, but continuing use has always been evident in the Orient and Greece. In the fifth century AD they were beginning to be used in Britain, after Knights returning from the Crusades, brought back recipes and ideas incorporating edible flowers.

Their uses now are limitless, pickles, teas, custards, stews, jams, honeys, salads, fritters, sauces, sorbets, vinegars to name but a few ... their colour, textures, tastes and postures in use of food and garnish are in many cases unbeatable ...

Always concern yourself with only picking or using flowers on buds where poisonous pesticides have not been used, never pick flowers you don't know or ones from florists or large nurseries where chemicals may have been used.

Pick them freshly in the morning and never use them if damaged by insects, fungi or disease. Double check each bud.

First wash the flowers in luke warm water and dry on kitchen paper, taking care not to damage the delicate petals.

My favourite flowers to cook with are carnations, jasmine, cowslips, lilac, roses, pansies, daisies, daffodils, nasturtiums, lavendar, primroses, chrysanthemums and apple blossoms.

The Black List of Flowers to Avoid:

Anenome	Hyacinth
Anthurium	Iris
Arum	Kalmia
Azalea	Laburnum
Bitter Stonecrop	Leopardsbane
Broom	Lily of the Valley
Bryony	Lupin
Buttercup	Meadow Rue
Callicarpa	Monkswood
Celandine	Mezereum
Cherry Laurel	Oleander
Rum Cherry	Paris Herb
Horsechestnuts	Pasque Flower
Rose of Christmas	Periwinkle
Clerodendron	Pheasants Eye
Clivia	Poppies
Cyclamen	Potato Plant
Deadly Nightshade	Rhubarb Leaves
Delphinium	Ragwort
Dieffenbachia	Rhododendron
Dwarf Elder	Rhus
Foxgloves	Safron Meadow
Friticary	St. John's Wort
Globe Flower	Snow Drop
Gloriosa	Snowflake
Greenweed	Spirea
Hemlock	Spurge
Henbane	Swallow Wort
Hepatica	Sweet Pea
Hogweed	Thorn Apple
Honeywort	

Inspirations and Influences

In the space of a few years I had worked in the kitchens of some of the most renowned chefs in the world and spoken to many.

Each one totally inspiring. Electrifying me with unforgettable experiences.

The calm, tranquility and ease of legendary Louis Outhier compared to Nico Ladenis, who also was a great influence on me. Yorkshireman Michael Quinn, whose philosophy of food and life are unforgettable. Vaughan Archer, firm, genial and eager, not forgetting Martin Davies, a true gentleman. Edward Hari, a great diplomatic character. Philip Corrick and Aidan McCormack. 'My daffodil conversation' with Ian McAndrew and the formidable Melvin Jordin. All had a great sense of humour and all had totally different characters.

You attempt to take the best from each man and his kitchen and formulate this, together with your own history and the various other chefs you have worked for and talked to, the names endless, during many years! 'mix in' yourself, and — Hey Presto!

Terminology of FOOD LANGUAGE

"It endlessly seems to amaze me the amount of 'Kitchen French' still religiously used today in your typical hotel kitchen. Why? To conceal and cloak our industry in secrecy, confusion and mystery? I have yet to hear of either English being used in French kitchens, or an English competitive restaurant springing up in gourmet areas of Europe.
Let's follow ourselves instead of the sheep of mumbo jumbo"

A la carte	individually priced cooked to order dishes
Au bleu	cooked under done
Au gratin	browned
Al dente	crisply cooked
A la crème	cream
Blanched	dipped into boiling water or oil
Bearnaise	hollandaise sauce with tarragon
Bain Marie	container of water for cooking in
Brunoise	small neat dice
Beurre blanc	white butter sauce
Clouté	studded onion with cloves
Carte de jour	menu of the day
Croutons	bread cut into shapes cooked in dill
Crepin	pigs caul
Concasse	coarsely chopped tomato or parsley
Crème chantilly	whipped cream with sugar and vanilla
De glacer	to swill out
Demi glace	reduce brown sauce
Farci	stuffing
Frit	fried
Flambé	to set light to
Fines Herbes	chopped herbs
Julienne	cut fine into strips
Jardiniere	cut into batons
Hollandaise	egg yolk and butter sauce
Les mille feuilles	thousand leaves, puff pastry cream slice
Liaison	egg yolks and cream to thicken
Le menu	bill of fare
Mornay	cheese style sauce
Mirepoix	rough cut clean vegetables
Misen en place	preparation
Macedoine	vegetable or fruit cut in 6mm dice
Noisette	slice cut from boneless meat
Napper	to coat with sauce
Provencale	tomato, garlic and onion sauce
Pané	to crumb
Purée	to strain or sieve
Paysanne	diced the size of a sixpence
Passer	to strain
Papillote	envelope
Reduce	to evaporate liquid to concentration
Polonaise	dry mix of butter, egg and crumb
Roux	fat and flour thickening agent
Refresh	plunge in ice water
Sauté	to toss or turn
Sweat	to cook with a lid on with no fat quickly without colour
Zeste	rind of lemon or orange

The Menu Contents

"Bread I leave to Bakers
As I leave Wines to Specialists" also ...

From a good classical training and background evolves a creative knowledge to make foods correctly and with taste.

Celery soup is made with celery, *why add onions?* Tomato soup is formed from tomatoes with a little carrot, *why add celery, onion and vast amounts of carrot to this?* And please, a mushroom soup needs 100% content of mushrooms, no vast barrage of vegetables to this.

Poor quality additions, left overs or bits are no formula for creating class soups, or really anything.

Stocks and sauces follow a similar route, clean fresh bones with knowledge will turn into the correct basis for the sauces. Stocks should be made as quickly as possible, sieved, cooled, used and consumed within a short period. The well known days of huge kitchen stock pots bubbling away for **days and all passers-by emptying all but** the kitchen sink in, are gone.

Starters and salads are first overall impressions of 'What's to Follow', colour, freshness and originality are the beginning to the menu.

Vegetables should be plain, simple and natural, very little evidence is needed of thick batters, ugly sauces, breadcrumbs or ghastly stuffings. Garlicing, braising or baking, it's an accompaniment to the main meal not a battle of colour, texture, taste and appearance. Does fresh poached salmon with dill suit battered cauliflower, stuffed mushrooms, duchesse potatoes and ratatouille? ... or fresh spinach, tiny new potatoes and fine green beans? The chapter enclosed on vegetables is for use, but as you feel fit — not gospel, horses for courses, please.

All meat and poultry needs to be fresh with good colour, road maps of Lincolnshire running through your sirloin will produce the expected result; the smell is also very important — pork suffering the colour of grey or yellow and sticky is for the receptical provided — not the dinner table! But please, for everyone's good, bite back! If products are not up to scratch return them to the seller. I'm sure he would return his flat pint if it was served in the bar.

It is as Nico Ladenis scorns a 'cliché' to enjoy cooking fish as a chef, and he would also criticise me for stating that my mother first taught me to cook, but he's like that and he is a pinacle for us all ... so to fish, my real deep down thoughts have always been (if you can imagine) the fish leaping from the water of the sea into a box and being delivered gleaming life-like but motionless, with fresh smells of the sea and eyes bright and glass-like — that's good fish.

The dessert and sweet is the 'Finale' and as important as any course. My chocolate plant pots for my chrysanthemum flowers, I must admit, were thought of whilst watching 'Bill and Ben the Flower Pot Men'!

The Cheeseboard, British ... and Proud of it ... from nook and crannies here there and everywhere from Thixendale to Wales, Cornwall, Cumbria and Devon, crisp celery, raddish, walnut bread, grapes, a few wheat wafers and maybe a vintage port or two ... the night is young!

John Benson Smith

ST. GEORGES DAY

English Canapes of Mrs. De Salis

—::—

Potato and Bacon Soup

Salamagundi

Smoked Loin of Pork with Celery Salad and Orange

—::—

Filey Cobble Stew

Roast Leg of English Lamb and Crab Stuffing
with Pease Pudding

Sussex Chicken and Leek Pie

Boiled Helmsley Silverside of Beef
and Parsley Dumplings

—::—

Almond and Apricot Crumble

Devonshire Junket

Mrs. Beetons Chocolate Souffle

Poor Knight's Pudding with Raspberries

—::—

Cheeses of England with Apples and Celery

Helmsley Fruit Cake and Wholemeal Scones

MENU FOR JANUARY
MAGIC OF FRANCE

In the style of Louis Outhier, Restaurant L'Oasis, La Napoule
by John Benson Smith

An ability to experiment is evident in success, some changes are necessary with stages
of evolution.
The collection for this month carries the secrets along with determination and knowledge
in a true result of mixing old and new, modern and tradition with styles and techniques
learnt and formulated in one of France's top Three Star Michelin rated Restaurants.

Oeuf de Brut L'Escargot
'Egg with Snails Eggs

—::—

Petit Casselette de Saint Jacques
small casselette of scallops

—::—

Cherry Marnier Sorbet

—::—

Steak de Canard à L'Orientale
Breast of Duck in Oriental Style

—::—

Brie Aux Truffle
French Brie with Truffle
served with a glass of Port

—::—

Petit Fours et Cafe

THE SEASON OF SAINT NICHOLAS
MENU FOR DECEMBER

by John Benson Smith

As a young apprentice, each year I would send friends a Christmas and New Year Card, inside I always wanted to enclose a recipe or menu, one of outstanding and meaningful simplicity, but also one of essential and dominant flavours and refinement. Now the feat is possible ... I dedicate this rustic, seasonal and inspiring festive menu for December.

The ideal marriage of classical and modern, keeping tradition alive.

Pea, Salmon and Potato Soup

— ∴ —

Moor Game Salad
with Gooseberry Champagne Dressing

— ∴ —

Whole Baked Baby Chicken in a Shell of Salt Paste
removed for presentation and service
with a thin Elderberry Pan Gravy

— ∴ —

Vegetables and Potatoes in Season

— ∴ —

Bread, Brandy and Plum Pudding
with Sherry Custard
served with a glass of Apricot Liqueur

'A twig of holly is placed on top to ward away witches in the night'

— ∴ —

This menu received an award from the Caterer and Hotelkeeper Magazine

THE COLOURS OF AUTUMN MENU
FOR OCTOBER

by Joanne Ward

A gathering of textures, tastes and colours inspired me whilst planning my menu ... the end of the Summer ... the beginning of Winter. The transitional period of Autumn. A joy to create.

Lobster, Avocado and Mango Salad
with Sherry Dressing

— ∴ —

Crab and Scallop Mousse

— ∴ —

Fresh English Guinea Fowl
with Yellow Wine and Wild Mushrooms

— ∴ —

Caramelised Pear with Lime
set in a Pastry Case with Berries and served
with a glass of Pere William

— ∴ —

GOURMET MENU OF OCTOBER

Trio of Salmons with Caviar

—::—

Cream of Wild Mushroom Soup

—::—

Hotch Potch of Sorbets

—::—

Fillets of Scotch Beef with Port

—::—

Cornish Yarg, Brie with Truffles
and Walnut Bread

—::—

Caramel Souffle in Brioche
with Chocolate Bavarian Cream

GASTRONOMIC MENU OF OCTOBER

Lobster and Asparagus Salad
with Emulsion of Egg Yolks, Snails Eggs and Caviar

—::—

Game Consomme

—::—

Hot Souffle of Lemon Sole, Ginger and Lime

—::—

Sorbet of Elderflowers

—::—

Terrine of Ratatouille
Foie Gras and Truffle

—::—

Fillet of Scotch Beef
with a Sauce of Port and Wild Mushrooms

—::—

Fresh Baked Figs
with Apricot Parfait and Mango Puree
presented in a Sugar Basket

GASTRONOMIC MENU FOR JUNE

Terrine of Local Rabbit with Madeira Jelly

— :: —

Prawn and Lobster Bisque with Tapioca

— :: —

Salad of Wild Mushrooms and Sweetbreads

— :: —

Roast Monkfish with Sorrel

— :: —

White Port Sorbet

— :: —

Supreme of English Duck
with Granny Smith Apples and Cassis

— :: —

Honey Wafers with Fresh Figs
Wild Strawberries and Rhubarb Sauce

FEAST OF FLOWERS MENU

The daffodils and flowers at Farndale overwhelmed me and started my intrigue and fascination with their beauty and taste when incorporated into Olde English Recipes and Medications.
Like all fashions in food the popularity of these recipes has diminished, but is now slowly and quietly being revived.
As composer, Sir John Goss wrote "O Taste and See".
John Benson Smith

Caviar with Egg and Daisies

— :: —

Forest Salad and Dandelions

— :: —

Rose Petal Sorbet with Caraway Seed Biscuits

— :: —

Daffodil in a Chocolate Pot with Pineapple Puree

FEAST OF FLOWERS MENU

The courteous meadows and woods of the Garden, romantic, full of grace, with meandering scents of colour.
The budding nursery of Cuisine, two streams mingle, a joy of creation.
John Benson Smith

Warm Flower Soup with Flocked Cream

— :: —

Raspberry and Violet Sorbet
with Crystallised Petals

— :: —

Strips of Chicken with Elderflower

— :: —

Summer Pudding with Rosepetals

FEAST OF FLOWERS MENU

Cuisine is a great art of inspiration, technique and intuition. Rich in perfection, the basis never ignored.
Flowers inspired Poets, Artists and Lovers. Pretty, delicate, simple — centuries old.
John Benson Smith

Warm Skillet of Mint and Cheese
Flower Cakes

— :: —

Roast Salmon with Nasturtiums
fine Caviar and Marigold Dressing

— :: —

Charcoaled Rose soaked English Duckling
with Pink Champagne

— :: —

Violet and Lemon Leaf Brulee
with Cherry Sauce and Pistachio Ice Cream

MENU OF DESSERTS
FROM THE PASTRY KITCHEN OF THE BLACK SWAN

Chocolate and Brandy Cake
made from an original Hotel Recipe with Chocolate Fudge Sauce

Pear Julia
A caramelised poached pear served in a puff pastry case with a Lime Sauce

Trio of Chocolate Mousses
made from Pink, White and Brown Chocolates

Apple Tart
Baked individually with English Apples

A Hot Strawberry Souffle
baked in a Sweet Pastry Mould (Please allow 10-15 minutes for this dessert)

Array of fresh Exotic Fruits
in season, with syrup

A Biscuit Sponge
with poached Meringue and Raspberry Sorbet
set on a pool of Fruit Coulis

A Savoury of Anchovies and Scrambled Eggs on Toast

Ice Creams of
Lemon & Coconut, Strawberry, Chocolate, Vanilla & Pistachio

Sorbets of
Blackcurrant and Cassis, Orange and Grand Marnier,
Drinking Cocolate, Apple and Calvados, Rosepetal and Elderflower

CHEESES

A selection of the finest quality cheeses
from the trolley including

Devon Garland
Made on Exmoor, this unpasteurised, unique cheese is blended with secret herbs

Wedmore
Made in Somerset. This is light with low fat content, flavoured with Chives

Tournegus
Made in Kent. It is similar to Caerphilly.
Washed in English Wine during manufacturing

Pencarreg
Made in Dyfed, Wales. Rich, Mellow and strong using organic milk

Yarg
Made in Cornwall (from Prince Charles' Estate). It is wrapped in nettles.
Ripens inwardly, a rich cheese

BEAUJOLAIS MENU

I have created this menu to celebrate what proves to be an exceptional Beaujolais Nouveau.

The dishes are light and in my opinion will perfectly complement the fresh young wine.

Beaujolais Nouveau Jaboulet Verchevre
Four Courses, inclusive of Coffee

— :: —

Salade 'Plaisir'
A Warm Winter Salad with yellow Pleurel Mushrooms,
Artichoke Bottoms and Asparagus

— :: —

Consomme de Saumon aux Julienne Poireaux
Served with brioche Croûtons and Sauce 'Rouille'

— :: —

Filet d'Agneau 'Corraine'
Fillet of English Lamb with a Sauce of Shallots and Wild Garlic
served with Macaire Potatoes and Mange Tout

— :: —

Assiette des Fruits au Beaujolais
A Basket of Fresh Fruits cured in Beaujolais with
Loganberry Water Ice and Blackcurrant Pancake

— :: —

GASTRONOMIC EXPERIENCE
12th - 13th MAY

Light Jelly of Salmon and Chives
crowned with Sour Cream and Caviar

— :: —

Clear Chicken Bouillon
garnished with Raviolis and parcels of Foie Gras

— :: —

Poached knots of local Dover Sole
with Coriander Scented Nage

— :: —

Elderflower Sorbet

— :: —

Spring Lamb
presented in three ways

— :: —

Warm Raspberries
nestled in a biscuit masked with Kirsch
served with Vanilla Pod Ice Cream and Angels Hair

— :: —

GARDNER MERCHANT
DINNER, 19th MAY

Caviar with Egg

— :: —

Poached Panaché of Fish with Vegetable Stock and Truffle

— :: —

Warm Salad of Asparagus, Avocado, Duck and Tomato

— :: —

Elderflower Sorbet

— :: —

Medallions of local Venison
with Ragout of Wild Mushrooms and Stuffed Vegetables

— :: —

Warm Blackberry Soufflé with Vanilla Pod Ice Cream

— :: —

Green Apples and Calvados Sauce

— :: —

Coffee

DINNER, 20th MAY

Warm Lobster Strudel with Butter Sauce

— :: —

Scallops Oriental

— :: —

Clear Chicken Consommé with fresh Pasta

— :: —

Rose Petal Sorbet

— :: —

Fillet of Beef with Foie Gras and Madeira and Fru Fru

— :: —

Brie with Truffles

— :: —

Raspberry Charlotte with Rosehip Syrup

— :: —

Coffee

GASTRONOMIC JUNE MENU

Oeuf au Caviar

— :: —

Cream of Cherry Tomato Soup

— :: —

Pastry of Fresh Truffle
with Foie Gras

— :: —

Elderflower Sorbet

— :: —

Roulade of Loch Fyne Salmon

— :: —

Medallions of Beef Fillet Perigeaux

— :: —

Trio of Chocolate Mousses

— :: —

Real English Countryside Cheeses

— :: —

SATCHI & SATCHI

John Benson Smith cooked the Dinner with the Brigade in
The Swan Hotel, Lavenham

English Canapés of Mrs. De Salis
— :: —

Œuf Au Caviar
— :: —

Salade Gourmande
— :: —

Mille Feuille of Loch Fyne Salmon
— :: —

Sorbet à L'eau de Rose
— :: —

Terrine of Duckling
and Pistachio Nuts
— :: —

Fillets of Beef Gowerdale
with Pru Pru
— :: —

A Small Selection of
Sweet Delicacies
— :: —

BEST OF BRITISH MENU FOR APRIL

by Nigel Wright, Sauce Chef

Savoury Lancashire Tasty Rolls
— :: —

Warm Salmon and Raisin Salad
— :: —

Mrs. Mill's Sup and Barley Soup
— :: —

Pleated Chicken with Cider and Apple Sauce
— :: —

Goose Gog and Carrot Pie
— :: —

Cheese from the Board
of an English Country House

BEST OF BRITISH MENU FOR MAY

Little Fish Sandwiches with Pickled Walnuts
— :: —

Soften Fancy with Quins Sauce
— :: —

Chilled Plum Soup
— :: —

Rump Steak and Potato Pudding with Sage Sauce
— :: —

Orange Custard Fitters with Apple Water
— :: —

Cheese from the Board
of an English Country House

A few of my

FAVOURITE BOOKS

John Benson Smith (portrait by Fiona Scott)

I RECOMMEND:

DICTIONARY OF COOKERY
    Cassel (1899)

FEAST OF FLOWERS
    Ian McAndrew

DINING IN FRANCE
    Christian Millau

GASTRONOMY
    Nico Ladenis

ON FOOD AND COOKING
    Harold McGee

COOKING WITH FLOWERS
    Greet Buchner

BEST OF BACON COOK BOOK
    Norman Manderson

LE REPERTOIRE DE LA CUISINE
    L. Saulnier

MASTER CHEFS OF GREAT BRITAIN
COOK BOOK
    David & Charles

MRS. BEETON'S FAMILY COOKERY
(1869)

FOOD IN YORKSHIRE
    Joan Poulson

CUISINE OF THE SUN
    Roger Verse

THE FISH COURSE
    Susan Hicks

CUISINE SPONTANÉE
    Fredy Girardet

MA CUISINE DES SAISONS
    George Blanc

GREAT DISHES
    British Gastronomic Academy

Also books by

John Tovey
Jane Grigson
Anton Mossiman
Elizabeth David
Roux Brothers

... and many I have forgotten

My many thanks to those who helped and assisted in making this book possible.